*The*
*Meaning*
*of Christ*

*by*
Robert Clyde Johnson

LAYMAN'S
THEOLOGICAL
LIBRARY

THE WESTMINSTER PRESS

PHILADELPHIA

PRINTED IN THE UNITED STATES OF AMERICA.

## CONTENTS

**6**

*Contents*

The religious book market is full of books for "the intelligent layman." Some are an insult to his intelligence. Others are covertly written for professional theologians. A few are genuine helps in communicating the faith.

In this spate of books being thrust at the lay reader, what distinctive place can the Layman's Theological Library claim to hold? For one thing, it will try to remind the layman that he *is* a theologian. The close conjunction of the words "layman" and "theological" in the title of the series is not by chance but by design. For theology is not an irrelevant pastime of seminary professors. It is the occupation of every Christian, the moment he begins to think about, or talk about, or communicate, his Christian faith. The injunction to love God *with all his mind* necessarily involves the layman in theology. He can never avoid theology; if he refuses to think through his faith, he simply settles for inferior theology.

Furthermore, the Layman's Theological Library will attempt to give a *wholeness* in its presentation of the Christian faith. Its twelve volumes cover the main areas of Christian faith and practice. They are written out of similar convictions which the authors share about the uniqueness of the Christian faith. All the authors are convinced that Christian faith can be made relevant, that it can be made understandable without becoming innocuous, and that (particularly in view of the current "return to religion") it is crucially important for the layman to commit himself to more than "religion in general." The Layman's Theological Library, then, will attempt a fresh exploration of the Christian faith, and what it can mean in the life of twentieth-century man.

The question, " What think ye of Christ? " (Matt. 22:42), is a question that no Christian can finally avoid. Sooner or later he must come to grips with it or abandon the pretense of being a Christian.

At a critical point in his ministry Jesus put the question to his disciples in two somewhat different ways. First of all, he asked them, " Who do men say that I am? " (Mark 8.27). This book gives us help in understanding better just what other men have said about the meaning of Christ.

But to leave the matter there would be to miss the point, as so many people do miss the point by letting their understanding of Christ remain academic. Jesus himself clearly saw the danger of this, for he went on to ask his followers a second question, a question that cannot be answered by reporting other peoples' opinions. He put it bluntly and directly: " Who do *you* say that I am? " (Mark 8:29). This one cannot be dodged. It cannot be answered with somebody else's answer. It demands our answer.

And it is in dealing with this second question that THE MEANING OF CHRIST will be of special help. For this book makes clear that an answer to Jesus' first question can never be a conclusion to the matter. It can only be a transition to the second question. The person who reads the following pages will make the disturbing, but exhilarating, discovery that the usual, conventional answers he has given even to the second question don't quite measure up. They have to be rethought. And the final answer the reader works out for himself may not be about a " gentle Jesus, meek and mild." But it will be about a Christ with power to save.

ROBERT MCAFEE BROWN

# 1

## IN THE BEGINNING GOD . . .

What image flashes across your mind when you think about God? A newspaper columnist who was pushed on this question by one of his readers acknowledged that he visualized " a sacred blur." One prominent theologian insists that we must think of " being as such," which is a more concrete blur. The child often thinks of an old man, sometimes with a long white beard. Each of us does think something, which means that we think *some thing*. What do *you* see with the eye of the mind when you think about God?

Our difficulties trace initially to the fact that words are like road signs. They point, but they have no meaning in themselves. They take on meaning only as we can visualize what they represent, or only when we have arrived at the destination to which they point.

There is, for example, nothing at all sacred about the word " God" as such. It is merely three letters, and if they are arranged differently, they spell " dog." The meaning is not in the word. It is in what we associate with the word, or in what we bring with us when we see or hear it.

The consequence is that if we bring little or nothing to the word " God," it can mean little or nothing to us. A typical religious interlude in one of the novels of Aldous Huxley italicizes this fact. In *Those Barren Leaves,* a Miss Thriplow,

who is between affairs, is suddenly smitten by a sense of
seriousness and an uneasy feeling that she should be more
" spiritual." The story relates how she " got into bed, and lying
on her back, with all her muscles relaxed, she began to think
about God." Her musings follow:

*God is a spirit, she said to herself, a spirit, a spirit. She tried
to picture something huge and empty, but alive. A huge flat
expanse of sand, for example, and over it a huge blank dome
of sky; and above the sand everything should be tremulous
and shimmering with heat — an emptiness that was yet alive.
A spirit, an all-pervading spirit. God is a spirit. Three camels
appeared on the horizon of the sandy plain and went lollop-
ing along in an absurd ungainly fashion from left to right.
Miss Thriplow made an effort and dismissed them. God is a
spirit, she said aloud. But of all animals camels are really almost
the queerest; when one thinks of their frightfully supercilious
faces, with their protruding underlips like the last Hapsburg
kings of Spain. . . . No, no; God is a spirit, all-pervading,
everywhere. All the universes are made one in him.*

If this seems somewhat ridiculous, what do *you* think when
you think about God?


## On the Ragged Edge of Blasphemy

If the Christian church is right, the significance of Jesus
Christ begins for us when we ask this question. Oddly enough,
the church insists that the question of the meaning of God,
and the question of the meaning of Christ, are *one* question —
or that the question of the meaning of Christ *is* the question
of the meaning of God. The purpose of the church is to bring
all men under the sovereign rule of the sovereign God, the
" Lord of heaven and earth." Its seemingly oblique approach
to this task is to ask us to divert our attention from sacred

blurs (and from camels, and "being as such"), and fix it steadily upon this man Jesus, an Oriental carpenter who lived briefly, and died violently, two thousand years ago.

The astounding contention of the church (which *ought* to jar us, and does jar us if we consistently refuse to domesticate it) is that the meaning that we bring to the word "God" must be the meaning that we find in this carpenter. It insists that every other path to God leads into boggy marshes from which we never emerge. "All thought about God which does not proceed from the fact of Christ is a fathomless abyss," said the sixteenth-century Reformer, John Calvin.

This is advice that should not be taken lightly, or accepted too quickly. To confuse a man with God — if it *were* confusion — would be about as confused as you could get. This is at once the most stupendous claim, and the most audacious claim, that has ever been made. In fact, at best it leaves us hanging on the ragged edge of blasphemy.

The Biblical writers placard this claim in many different ways, but the expressions used by John and Paul are sufficient to suggest its presumption. John speaks of the man Jesus as "the Word" of God, God's self-communication or message. (John 1:1-18.) His expression carries more meaning than we ordinarily would give it, however, because he clearly identifies Jesus, the "message" God has sent, with God himself.

"The Word *was* God," he says. "He was in the beginning with God; all things were made through him, and without him was not anything made that was made." John obviously is suggesting that Jesus was in some sense the personal, *self-*communication of God, or that *in this man God was himself appearing, acting, and speaking* in human life and history. "No one has ever seen God," he says; *but* "the only Son, who is in the bosom of the Father, he has made him known."

Paul makes essentially the same claim. "God was *in* Christ,"

he says, " reconciling the world to himself." (II Cor. 5:19.)
The word " Christ," in Paul's Greek, represents a Hebrew
word that means " anointed." The Hebrew word also may be
translated " Messiah." The Messiah, or Christ, was " the
anointed of the Lord." It is important to remember this, because it means that implicitly the heart of the Christian claim
is present if we speak the words " Jesus Christ." " Jesus " is a
name, but " Christ " is a title. The word itself is a confession
of faith. To say " Jesus Christ " is at the least to say that the
man Jesus was " the anointed of the Lord."

Paul is saying even more than this, however. He insists that
God was "*in*" Christ, that in this carpenter God was himself personally present. His contention is that *here God did
something that entirely changed the relationship of man to
himself.* We shall examine the astonishing implications of this
claim in Chapter 3. But it is obvious on the face of it that
Paul is saying nothing less than that in this carpenter from
Nazareth the Lord of heaven and earth invaded history and
changed its course, that at this *one* time, in this *one* place, in
this *one* man, God " reconciled " the world to himself.

The Christian church, Protestant, Roman Catholic, and
Orthodox, has carried forward this contention. The Reformers
of the sixteenth century quarreled with many things in the
sixteenth-century church, but they stood squarely upon both
the Bible and the ancient creeds. They affirmed, as virtually
all Christians have always (officially) affirmed, that this man
Jesus who appeared in Palestine in the first century was, in
phrases from the Nicene Creed, " God of God; Light of Light;
Very God of Very God."

When we are aware that the cutting edge of its creed is this
sharp, it is not difficult to understand why there always have
been some who have charged Christianity with blasphemy. It
actually adds up to this:

If the Christian claim about this man Jesus is *true,* his appearance in Palestine in the first century manifestly was the most momentous event in all human history.

If this claim is *not true,* we can only conclude that the Christian church is living under a gigantic illusion, hoax, and blasphemy.

The issue should not be less sharply drawn. It is not less sharp.

## Toward Letting God Be God

This is why it is so essential in any discussion of the meaning of Christ to guard from the outset against two easily committed errors:

1. We must not attempt, consciously or unconsciously, to make Christ another god beside God.

2. We must in no way, consciously or unconsciously, try to substitute him for God.

We shall discuss in Chapter 4 the means by which the church has attempted to avoid these errors, and also the meaning and the limits of the creedal assertion that he was "Very God of Very God." But here we must, from the first, take a firm stand on a prior point that is crucial and all-pervasive, the point that there is *one* God, and *only* one.

It is an unquestionable fact of history that Christianity has affirmed from its birth that God is "the Father Almighty" (the Apostles' Creed). The church has fought a life-and-death battle against every suggestion that there could be two gods, or that Jesus was or is a second god. We must remember that — whatever else he may have been — Jesus was Hebrew, and had his feet planted firmly on Hebrew soil. The roots of the church were sunk deeply in this same soil. The one word to which the Hebrew clung beyond all others was, "I am the Lord thy God; . . . thou shalt have no other gods before me." This was the *first* commandment, and it remained the first commandment.

The Shema (the word means " Hear ") was the " creed " of Judaism. It was the first scripture taught to Jewish children, and it was recited every morning and evening. It begins:

" Hear, O Israel: The Lord our God is *one Lord;* and you shall love the Lord your God with all your heart, and with all your soul, and with all your might. And these words which I command you this day shall be upon your heart; and you shall teach them diligently to your children, and shall talk of them when you sit in your house, and when you walk by the way, and when you lie down, and when you rise." (Deut. 6:4-7.)

Nothing could be surer, from the point of view (*a*) of its heritage, (*b*) of the Biblical material, (*c*) of the creeds of Christendom, or (*d*) of the history of the church, than that belief in *one* God (known technically as monotheism) is the primal presupposition of Christianity.

This clearly fences in every quest for the meaning of Christ. If we examine the lay of the land within this fence, we find that if the question of the meaning of Christ is correctly asked *we must in reality be asking about the attitude, the intent, and the action of God.* God is God; and he must remain our God, even as we respond to Christianity's invitation to fix our attention singularly upon Christ. Hence we can respond to this invitation, and avoid superstition and blasphemy in so doing, only if from beginning to end it is the *one God* we seek.

It is this clear limitation which poses both our first and our last problem. If we acknowledge one God, recognizing with the Apostles' Creed that he is " the Father Almighty," it is obvious that our *undivided* allegiance belongs to him. Our concern must be directed *to God,* even as we seek the meaning of Christ.

At the same time, however, it is a simple fact that Christianity has always concentrated its attention and its concern upon Jesus, this man of flesh and blood who lived and died "under Pontius Pilate." The problem thus becomes: *is it possible to focus our attention both upon God, and upon this man, without losing sight of either?* If this *is* possible, can it be done without developing a kind of theological astigmatism, in which one is blurred when we look toward the other? This is what we may call "the optical problem" of Christianity. We must examine it more closely.

## The Optical Problem

There is a revealing episode in the Fourth Gospel which suggests that this problem caused no small amount of trouble even for the disciples of Jesus. Philip said to Jesus, "Lord, show us the Father, and we shall be satisfied." The startling reply, which must have shaken Philip to his very foundations, was: "He who has seen me has seen the Father; how can you say, 'Show us the Father'?" (See John 14:8-9.)

Jesus here is pointing up the tragic fact that when we seek to understand him, or when we seek to understand God, it is very easy to see without seeing. Among his more pathos-ridden words recorded in the Gospels is the observation that he was forced to make about the crowds who followed him: "seeing they do not see" (Matt. 13:13).

This is the optical problem which we find hovering over every quest for the meaning of Christ, if there is a (necessary) sharp consciousness that there are "no other gods" before or beside God. If in looking to Jesus our attention is diverted from God, we have blundered on one side. Or if we attempt to "see God" without looking to Jesus, we have blundered on the other. To blunder on either side is to see without seeing.

A clue to the kind of optical dexterity that is required of us, if we are in any measure to avoid these blunders, is unwittingly suggested by Ortega y Gasset, in a critical essay that he wrote on modern art some years ago. He suggested that the knack which we must master in order to appreciate contemporary painting is symbolized by the experience of looking through a window at a garden.

Optically it is possible to do either of two things. We may focus upon the window. If we do so, we see the garden; but it is only a confused mass of color pointlessly framed by the window. If, however, we focus upon the garden, we not only see the garden clearly, and appreciate it fully, but we also see the window as it should be seen. The function of a window is transparency; and the more transparent it is the more perfectly it fulfills its reason for being. It is when we see *through* a window that we see a window as it is intended to be seen.

It is in much the same way that we must look to Jesus Christ when we seek to fathom his meaning. It must be axiomatic that *God* is God. If our concern with this man Jesus in any way distorts this fact, we have tumbled into the optical fallacy and violated the basic conviction of the Christian faith, that there is *one* God. Yet, if the New Testament is right in its claim that "God was in Christ," we may, and we *must*, turn to this man with complete and final concern. It must be, however, a looking " through " Jesus to see God, as we would look through a window to see a garden. This is the only conceivable rationale, and the only defensible justification that we could have, for a life-and-death preoccupation with a first-century carpenter.

There is one other — even deeper — level in this problem. What do we mean when we speak of " looking to Jesus " or of "looking at Jesus "? Does it make any sense to talk this way? Obviously he is no longer here in the flesh. Nor has he been for two thousand years. Is it any more than nonsense to talk as though he were? Or is it possible that we could " see " him no better if he were visible in the flesh?

Sören Kierkegaard, a provocative Danish Christian of the nineteenth century, raised the fascinating question as to whether the original disciples (" the disciple at first hand ") had any decisive advantage over us (" the disciple at second hand "). We commonly assume that they did. But did they?

The New Testament report of the first confession that Jesus was " the Christ " speaks volumes to this question. It was made by the disciple Peter. Jesus asked, " Who do you say that I am? " Peter answered, " You are the Christ, the Son of the living God." In response Jesus observed, " Flesh and blood has not revealed this to you, but my Father who is in heaven." (See Matt. 16:13-20.)

These words expose to our view the deepest level of Christianity's optical problem. The only literal sense in which we today can " look at Jesus " is by reading of him in the New Testament or in other books that draw upon the New Testament. But if the men who lived and worked with him could not " see " his meaning when they could see him in the flesh, how can we hope to do so just by looking at a word picture of him, or by reading about him in a book?

The answer is that *we cannot* — and this answer must be taken with complete seriousness. Martin Luther's pithy way of expressing this crucial acknowledgment was, " God hid in the despised man Christ." What Jesus was saying to Peter was that his meaning as " the Christ " must be " revealed " by God. The word " reveal " means " unveil " or " disclose." To say that something must be revealed is to say that it is not available to our search — or to our research. It must be unveiled *for* us, or disclosed *to* us. To say that the meaning of Christ must be revealed by God is to say that *only God* can do the disclosing or unveiling. Otherwise, his real meaning remains " veiled " to us. Where does this necessary conclusion lead us?

### Understanding Christ = " Standing Under " Christ

Among other things it raises the pertinent question of whether any book on the meaning of Christ is worth what we pay for it. It may be too late now to try for a refund on this one; but it should be kept in mind in reading this or any other book on Christ that to assume that his meaning can be found in a book, even in the Bible, is one of the quickest ways to become embroiled in the optical problem.

This does not mean, however, that God does not *use* the Bible in unveiling the meaning of Christ to us. Nor does it mean (as it is rather fashionable at the moment to assume) that *the man Jesus,* as the Bible pictures him for us, is not important. It was *in* and *through* this man of flesh and blood that God disclosed himself; and it is *in* and *through* the Biblical word picture of him that God discloses himself to us today.

Since this word picture is essential, it is apparent that if God is to disclose himself to us, we must *understand* what is disclosed. When we concede that this understanding is possible only as God reveals himself, we have conceded that it is a unique kind of understanding. It is different in kind from what ordinarily is required of us when we set our heads to master some subject. The difference is suggested by the simple-minded observation (which is so simple-minded that it frequently is overlooked — except by the simple-minded) that in its most literal sense " to understand " means " to stand under." Few things, whether simple-minded or not, could be as important to us when we are trying to fathom the meaning of Christ.

For this is the sense in which Christ *must* be " understood."

And it is the only sense in which he *may* be understood. When we read a biography of Julius Caesar, or of Winston Churchill, nothing more is demanded of us than a reasonable ability to understand what the words mean. But this is not true when we read about Jesus Christ. He demands not only the insight of our minds, but also the allegiance of our lives. And correct understanding *of* him depends upon this allegiance *to* him. It can come in no other way. Here to " understand " means to " stand under," to give him our complete allegiance.

We may wish that it were otherwise, but it is not. The first words that Jesus spoke, when he " came into Galilee, preaching the gospel of God," were the words " repent " and " believe." (See Mark 1:14-15.) Both words underscore the point. " Repent " means turn about. It is a movement in which we shift our position, so that we are facing in a different direction. Until we are — with our whole lives — facing in *his* direction, the meaning of Christ remains hidden from us.

The word that here is translated " believe " means to trust or have confidence. It is not something that we can do just with our heads. In his terms, we " believe " with the whole of our lives or we do not believe. And except as we make this movement of trust, the meaning of Christ remains veiled to us.

The point could not be clearer. The meaning of Christ is disclosed to us only as we offer him our lives. " In *this* knowing we are not the masters but the mastered," says Karl Barth, the great Swiss theologian. We must " stand under " the message that God unveils in Christ in order to " understand " it. In other areas of life it is neither necessary nor desirable always to take personally what someone says to us. Understanding Christ is uniquely different. We must take him personally or we do not understand him at all.

## 2

## THE MAN JESUS

The story of the man Jesus has been recorded for us in the first books of the New Testament, the writings that we call "Gospels." The first three of these (called the "Synoptic" Gospels, because they can be studied "synoptically," or in parallel columns) differ from the other New Testament books in that they are less concerned to explore in detail the meaning of Christ. Their concern is more to record, in rapid-fire order, accounts of his life, teaching, death, and resurrection, and the varying responses to him of his disciples, the multitude, the leaders of Judaism, and the officials of the state.

They are not objective "biographies," in the modern sense of this word. They were written within the church, by believers, and for the express purpose of presenting Jesus as the Christ, or the Messiah. They plainly are, in the best sense of the word, "propaganda." But even so, their preoccupation is more with the events through which the meaning of Christ was disclosed than with that meaning itself. They leave it to the other New Testament books to take care of the latter task.

### Attraction and Repulsion

When we read this succinct, synoptic story with a serious eye, it has a double-edged effect upon us, just as the presence of Jesus had a double-edged effect upon those who encountered him during his life. The man whom the story pictures both attracts and repels us. He arouses in us a certain admiration and longing, but also an uneasy anxiety and dread. He is presented, at one and the same time, and with almost uncanny success, as the most majestic and magnetic person in all of history, and as the most forbidding and accusing figure who has ever walked the earth.

Each of these two reactions to the man Jesus is equally important to a recognition of his meaning. If the Biblical claim that he was "the Word of God" is true, then to eliminate either the attraction or the repulsion, or to fail to take either seriously, will result, not only in a warped view of Jesus, but also in a warped conception of God.

The God who is disclosed through this man is a God of *holy love* — and each of these words is equally important. It was through the forbidding and accusing effect that Jesus had upon men that they came to recognize this love as *holy* love. The inviting aspects unveiled to them God's mercy and forgiveness, his holy *love*. In the same way, as the meaning of Christ is disclosed to us through the Gospels we find one side of the matter accusing us, and forcing us into a new appraisal of ourselves. We find the other side unveiling the forgiving intention of God toward this unmasked self.

In an attempt to throw these two sides in relief, we shall look at them separately. Their meaning actually cannot be separated in human experience, and each is only a half-truth apart from the other. This should be remembered throughout the present chapter, where we shall trace some of the forbidding and accusing strands of the story, and try to see how they force us to a new appraisal and estimate of ourselves. This is *only one side,* but we cannot understand the other side apart from it.

In Chapter 3 we shall turn to the other side of the picture, concentrating on the inviting aspects of the story and the message of forgiveness that they reveal. The two sides will be brought together in Chapter 4, when we turn directly to the confession of faith that the church makes about Jesus.

## The Accuser

Our modern age has suffered from a somewhat nauseating tendency to sentimentalize this story, until at times it is distorted almost beyond recognition. A few years ago one of the Protestant churches published a new hymnal for its children. The comment of one reviewer was significant, and applicable far beyond the confines of the little book which he was reviewing. " This book is preoccupied with lambs," he observed. " It will not be surprising if, when the children who have used this book reach adulthood, they see little lambs hopping by whenever they hear a reference to Christianity."

This symbolizes the curious fate that Christianity generally and the man Jesus in particular have suffered in modern hands. There has been a recurring suggestion that Jesus was velvety. We have come to assume almost unconsciously that there was a soft streak running through his personality. In most contemporary paintings of him, which are strewn freely, and without much thought, through the Sunday school rooms of Protestant churches, it would not be immediately apparent, except for the beard, whether he was male or female. He has been pictured so often, and for so long, as the " gentle Jesus, meek and mild " that the other half of the record — the side that repels — has been almost entirely forgotten.

One of our great needs at the moment is to be jarred into an awareness that this is not just a regrettable cultural phenomenon. It is a fatal distortion. There must be a good reason why the writers of the Gospels so carefully recorded the so-called " hard " sayings and deeds, and why the major share of their accounts is devoted to a minute description of the crucifixion and all the chilling horror surrounding it. The fact of the matter is that a failure to recognize this " hard " side of the story, and to see that the crucifixion (whatever else it may be) was a brutal, first-century way of getting rid of undesirables, really *prohibits* an insight into the meaning of Christ.

What do we find on this neglected side of the record? Some words of Stefan George are suggestive:

> " One man stood up who, sharp as steel and lightning,
>   Tore open clefts and separated camps,
>   Inverting your world, fashioned a beyond. . . ."

The bare truth is that here was a man who could be as hard as nails when the circumstances demanded it. He was a fearless revolutionary in his actions; and his words cut through the sham and hypocrisy of his day like " steel and lightning." There was a searing effect in his presence; and there was a cutting edge to his teaching.

The minimal facts of his public activity are quite simple. It began at the time of his baptism by John the Baptist, when he was approximately thirty years of age. We know virtually nothing about the years prior to this. The *early* months of his ministry were spent in the north, in his native Galilee. Here he gathered a band of followers, including an inner group of twelve disciples. He taught wherever he found hearers, and he healed wherever he found suffering. His mission almost immediately created opposition among professional religionists and self-appointed guardians of the faith, and after a comparatively brief period of popularity his following dwindled.

The *latter* part of his ministry was spent in and around

Jerusalem, in the south of Palestine. Here the antagonism and
bitterness were intensified, and the religious authorities determined to do away with him. He was betrayed by one of his
inner group and arrested by the Roman authorities. After
having been given perfunctory trials by both the religious and
the civil governments, he was condemned to death by crucifixion, and was crucified.

The span of time covered by these events is uncertain, and
any estimate depends upon technical questions of interpretation that are extremely difficult. But it appears certain that
the maximum possibility is three years, and the events could
have taken place in little more than one.

The predominant theme in this account, when it is viewed
factually, is the swift and bitter opposition that Jesus created.
His reaction to this opposition is no less a part of the story
than his quite different relationship to his disciples, to the
downcast and needy, and to the children he encountered.
And it is a very important part of the story, as we shall see.

The majority of the religious leaders had deified the *status
quo*. In the name of the preservation of truth and righteousness,
they had passed the point where they could entertain even a
slight degree of flexibility in their cherished customs and
traditions. They fought for, and enforced, " the law," even if
they inflicted hardship and suffering upon the people in so
doing.

Jesus' reaction to these leaders was not so " gentle, meek,
and mild." He looked them in the eye and bluntly called them
" blind fools " (Matt. 23:17). He condemned the very nature of
their righteous, religious crusade, and scorned its results. He
tersely remarked that when they won a convert they only
succeeded in making him " twice as much a child of hell "
(v. 15) as they themselves were.

This type of approach was hardly calculated " to win friends and influence people." It won him few friends, and it influenced the religious leaders only to turn solidly against him. He reacted to this opposition not by retracting, but by lucidly clarifying his charges, beyond all chance of misunderstanding. Repelled by the utter absence of compassion among those who professed to represent God to the people, and fearlessly calling a spade a spade, he flung the truth in their faces. He charged them with being "full of extortion and rapacity," "evil and adulterous," "faithless and perverse," a "brood of vipers," and "ravenous wolves." (Matt., chs. 7; 12; 17; and 23.) It would hardly have occurred to those who caught the thrust of these charges to suggest that this man was soft.

He also proved to be, when the circumstances called for it, a master of irony. When the "good church people" remained unmoved by his searing, direct words, they felt the thrust and the sharp point of the indirect and ironical. "Those who are well have no need of a physician, but those who are sick," he said; "I came not to call the righteous, but sinners." (Mark 2:17.)

The threat of sentimentalizing his intent, and of transposing it into a peace-of-mind sedative, was present in his time, as it is in ours. Some of his hardest sayings are directed at this utterly misleading kind of distortion. "I came," he said, "to cast fire upon the earth; and would that it were already kindled! . . . Do you think that I have come to give peace on earth? No, I tell you, but rather division." (Luke 12:49-51.)

To make thoroughly clear the astounding, absolute nature of the allegiance that he was demanding, he said, "If any one comes to me and does not hate his own father and mother and wife and children and brothers and sisters, yes, and even his own life, he cannot be my disciple" (Luke 14:26 — a verse rarely used as a Mother's Day text).

And lest those who did choose to give him their allegiance

should have naïve notions about the life that they were choosing, or about the world in which they would work, he said: "I send you out as sheep in the midst of wolves. . . . Brother will deliver up brother to death, and the father his child, and children will rise against parents and have them put to death; and you will be hated by all for my name's sake." (Matt. 10:16, 21, 22.)

There is little here that is velvety.

## The Crucifixion

The most telling fact of all, however, was his reaction to danger and the threat to his life. He very shortly provoked a group of antagonists who could be satisfied only with his death. The conviction seized him that he should carry his message south, to Jerusalem. Here he would have to deal not only with the religious leaders but also with the political forces, with men who held in their hands the power to do what the religious leaders were plotting to have done. It was a decision that was, in the most literal sense, a matter of life and death.

The disciples recognized the fatal danger implicit in the decision to go to Jerusalem. It was Peter, the rugged fisherman, who voiced their collective feelings on the matter. The story says that he " began to rebuke him, saying, ' God forbid, Lord! This shall never happen to you.'" The response of Jesus was as strong as any of his recorded words. " He turned and said to Peter, ' Get behind me, Satan! You are a stumbling-block to me; for you are not on the side of God, but of men.'" (See Matt. 16:21-23, margin.)

We are told that from this moment Jesus " set his face to go to Jerusalem," being fully conscious of the consequences. When he arrived, he spoke out fearlessly against the evil and corruption that he found there. He attacked the polluted order single-handedly, driving those who were profiteering within the sacrificial system from the Temple. (Mark 11:15-19.)

The inevitable happened. He was arrested and tried, derided and spat upon, slapped and beaten. The charge of blasphemy that the religious leaders brought against him was not a capital-punishment offense under the Roman rule. Consequently, in the end, the decision was forced upon a minor politician named Pilate, the Roman governor in Jerusalem. He bowed to the screams of a festival mob, and ordered Jesus scourged and executed in the place of a convicted murderer by the name of Barabbas.

This scourging was known as " the terrible preface." The law prohibited it for a Roman citizen; but it was often used, as a terror weapon, upon subjects in the colonies. Historical fragments describe it for us. Jesus was stripped, bound in a stooping position to a stake, and beaten with lashes that had sharp-pointed bones, or chips of metal, at the ends. He then was nailed to a wooden cross, the nails being driven through the flesh of his hands and feet. A spear was thrust into his side, and he was left to die in prolonged and unrelieved agony.

The account reveals clearly that there were numerous times when Jesus could easily have reversed his course and avoided this fate. The record is almost excessively candid in reporting that he not only thought of doing so, but wished to do so. The reason why he did not is also clearly pictured for us.

He was motivated by a deep-seated, consuming desire to do the will of God; and he was convinced that the path that he followed was the only one open to him if the will of God were to be done. (Matt. 26:36-46.) No consideration less weighty could explain the steel-like determination with which he pursued his course, and the unwavering finality of his decisions and actions in the face of certain suffering and death.

### "Oughtness" — Redefined

What effect do the steel-like qualities in this man have upon *us* today, two thousand years after?

The flourishes that we give it may be different, but the basic way of thinking that we bring to our meeting with him is not essentially different from that of his time. One of the queerest things about human life is the persistent, odd sense of "oughtness" that goes with being human. We have definite feelings that there are certain things that we "ought" to do, and that there are certain other things that we "ought not" to do. This was true two thousand years ago, and it remains true today.

There may be those who wish that this were not so, and there doubtless are times when *we* wish that it were not so; but it *is* so. You have your personal collection of "oughts" and "ought nots," and the man next door has his. Even the hardened criminal feels, with real conviction, that he "ought not" to rat on his accomplice. This is a part of life that is not easily explained; but it undeniably is a part of life, as every one of us knows.

There are some who insist that this is taught to us (or is wished upon us) by society. This may be true. It certainly is true that the culture in which we live in large part determines the content of our collection, the particular things that we feel we "ought" and "ought not" to do. The head-hunter feels that he "ought" to hunt heads — in his society it is a religious duty. The chances are that you feel that you "ought not" to hunt heads — at least not in the same sense that he does. This obviously is because you live in a society that does not practice the same kind of head-hunting.

But this does not explain *why* we should have this feeling of "oughtness." Nor does it explain it away. We sometimes call it " conscience," and it is so universal and persistent a part of human life that some of history's greatest thinkers have suggested that it is the distinguishing mark of man, or that this, beyond all else, sets man apart from the animal.

If there is any truth at all in this, it means two things: (1) that no man is without some conscience; (2) that if there were to be someone without this feeling of " oughtness," because of irrationality or some other reason, he would have ceased to be " man " in the full sense.

This we share with those who encountered Jesus. There is much of his teaching that we understand only when we know that in his time there had been a feverish attempt to standardize the mold that shapes this sense of " oughtness." This standard mold had been constructed of the six hundred and thirteen precepts of the ancient code of Judaism. The so-called " scribes " were the official trustees of the mold, and the people who were called " Pharisees " were its self-appointed watchdogs. The scribes were professional religionists. Concern for the religious code or " law " was their full-time occupation. The Pharisees originated as a lay " protestant " movement, organized for the express purpose of protesting against moral laxity. Their platform had one plank — that man " ought " to obey the law of God.

This may strike us as very " right " and " righteous," or as very " religious " — until we notice the disconcerting fact that Jesus would have no part of it. In fact, this " righteous " sensitivity was the sore spot that he touched, that accounted for the bitter resistance that he provoked.

The embarrassment was prompted by the fact that he had the audacity to probe under the neatly manicured surface of life, beneath the studied obedience to laws and precepts in which so many prided themselves. His words cut into the inner, secret areas, which had been cleverly hidden by this

polished outer behavior. It was there, in the hidden crevices
of life, that he found what necessitated the hard epithets —
"evil," "adulterous," "faithless," "perverse," "brood of
vipers," and "ravenous wolves" "full of extortion and rapacity." "You are like whitewashed tombs," he said, "which
outwardly appear beautiful, but within they are full of dead
men's bones and all uncleanness." (Matt. 23:27.)

Jesus then set about to recast completely man's feeling of
"oughtness." He did this by *reinterpreting the demand that
God makes upon us.* His reinterpretation was so radical that
he unavoidably became Man's Great Accuser.

This reinterpretation is both negative and positive in its
inner nature; that is, he completely recast both God's "ought
nots" and his "oughts."

He reinterpreted the demand of God negatively by unveiling
the heart of the law of God. This had the effect of turning
it in upon its very defenders. With its true, implicit meaning
he uncovered the hidden bent of life — the attitudes, motiva-
tions, and desires that are kept so carefully concealed from the
world. What this disclosed shook the scribes and Pharisees to
their depths, and his words shake us to our depths when we
really permit ourselves to be exposed to them.

In what we call the "Sermon on the Mount" the "I say to
you" passages (Matt., ch. 5) are the most pointed examples
of these accusing reinterpretations. "You have heard that it
was said to the men of old, 'You shall not kill; and whoever
kills shall be liable to judgment,'" he observes. The vast
majority of his hearers were not murderers, so could nod
their heads approvingly. This caused the average man of his
day little anguish, and most of us do not find it excessively
binding or particularly accusing.

"But *I say to you,*" he continues, "that every one who is
angry with his brother shall be liable to judgment." This is

something else. Here the law has become a scalpel, cutting to the heart of the matter. Now anger is moved under the same judgment as murder, as we are told that for our most hidden angry thoughts and inclinations we are as guilty before God as if we had killed someone in cold blood. How much does this leave us to say for ourselves?

Again the time-honored law said, "'You shall not commit adultery.'" Once more the average man, at least in the time of Jesus, could measure himself by the letter of the law and fare fairly well. Jesus adds, "But *I say to you* that every one who looks at a woman lustfully has already committed adultery with her in his heart."

We are (to put it mildly) somewhat less than eager to have adultery redefined in this way. Now the hidden thought, the slightest secret, lustful desire, is thrown with the overt act under a common judgment. It is painfully obvious that here the "ought" has been radically recast, and in an almost intolerable way. Who could escape this accusation? Brunner has remarked, "This makes every one of us an adulterer."

Again and again Jesus takes the bearable external regulation of the law, the old "ought not," and recasts it in such a way that it becomes unbearable — so that no one of us escapes condemnation. As long as we may make a Pharisaic judgment upon our lives, judging them by *our* interpretation of God's law, or by what *we* think we should be and do, our sense of "ought" is bearable. But what can we say when we have exposed ourselves to this shattering reinterpretation, and to the new demand of God that comes with it?

Jesus also redefined our sense of "oughtness" *positively*. The principal word that he used in doing so was "love." There was nothing new about this word, but there was something radically new about the content that he gave to it in his teaching and in the way he lived and died. We shall return to this in the next chapter; but here we should notice that this new meaning demanded a completely outgoing, uncalculated, and selfless concern for others, and without discrimination. "Love your enemies" marks the outer edge of the demand. Everything short of this, whatever might be our reasons for falling short, he brought under the judgment of God.

## The Great Accusation

What happens when this kind of demand is placed upon life? The first-century reaction was violent. As we look at the cross we see how violent. It will not be less violent today where people really listen to his accusing words. Here a sharp and probing knife has sliced through the tidy layers of pretense that we enfold about ourselves and has laid bare what no one of us can afford to have exposed — either to public *or* to private view. Here the locus of the inquiry has been shifted abruptly from our accepted, "acceptable" outer actions to that private inner chamber where we hide the thoughts and desires that we do not want to admit, even to ourselves, that we have. The demand placed upon life has been so radically redefined that no one upon whom these words fall can escape a sentence of condemnation. And the sentence is pronounced in the name of God!

Of course, this is a strange way of thinking to most of us today. Even if it were not, it would seem strange to associate it with Jesus. We have almost lost the ability to think of him except as our "Friend" (who walks "in the garden" with us), our "Helper," our "Elder Brother," our "Companion," "the Great Scoutmaster of all good scouts," or some such. It is all there in the record, however — the part of the record we have avoided reading, and of which we perhaps are not too happy to be reminded.

But this was also a strange way of thinking in Jesus' time. This is precisely the point. No man would presume to explore and expose the secret chamber of the life of another, and pronounce the judgment of God upon what he found there. It is only because we know that we are secure from this kind of intrusion that we can maintain sanity and a tolerable balance in life.

When we encounter Jesus he permanently upsets this balance. Sören Kierkegaard once observed that an adult may play with children and may enjoy doing so; but he plays as an adult, not as a child. In the same way, when we have been " matured " by an exposure to the great accusation that appeared in history when Jesus appeared in Palestine, we may continue in our childish ways. But we cannot do so without knowing that we are doing so, and without feeling our guilt.

This is why our initial encounter with this man is a jarring, threatening, repelling experience. He accuses us in a way that no man can accuse us. It is so profoundly disturbing (1) because the accusation is in the name of God, and (2) because we know that it is accurate. He forces us to look at every bleak blotch and dark shadow within, even those which we have managed to keep hidden from ourselves. He scrutinizes our most secret selves in a way that only God is capable of doing.

Friedrich Nietzsche, in *Thus Spake Zarathustra,* introduces one character who is called " the murderer of God." In his own defense he protests, " But he — *had* to die: he looked with eyes which beheld *everything,* — he beheld men's depths and dregs, all his hidden ignominy and ugliness." Zarathustra agrees, " Thou couldst not *endure* him who beheld *thee,* — who ever beheld thee through and through."

This is the effect that the life and words of the man Jesus had upon the men of his time. And it is the effect that he has continued to have, upon men of all time. His very presence was (and is) "The Great Accusation."

## God Is Holy

This is one of the two ways (distinguished on page 21) in which we may "see" God in looking to Jesus. For two thousand years men have discovered in their encounter with him what it means to say that *God is holy*. Face to face with Jesus, they have realized that this is no pious shibboleth, but that it involves a concrete acknowledgment that inevitably is followed by a painful recognition.

The acknowledgment is that in God, just because he *is* God, there can be no indulgence. The recognition is of the truth about ourselves, a truth that we can see and accept only as we view ourselves in the light of God's *holy* love. We need to explore each of these, as they relate to the meaning that Christ has for our lives.

1. *The acknowledgment.* This word "holy" is the opposite of "profane," which means "earthy" or "secular." The root of "holy," as Jesus used it, means "separate." The word "separate" is both an adjective (meaning "apart from") and a verb (meaning "to part"). This suggests the two aspects of the holiness of God that are unveiled in Christ.

When we confess that God is holy, if our confession means anything, we become sharply conscious that (in some pointed words of Emil Brunner) "God — alone — is God, the creature is — only — a creature." God is "Other"; he is "separate"; he is "far from us." When we confuse him with our ideas, ideals, and idols (such as "Americanism," "Democracy," "Segregation," "Peace of Mind," "Inner-Direction," "Self-realization," "Other-centeredness," etc.), and try to endorse them with his name, the god whom we worship is not God, but some god of our own devising. "God is in heaven, and you upon earth": this is one aspect of the holiness of God.

It is as this fact of our faith is seared upon our consciousness that we know that God stands, and *must* stand, in judgment "over against" — or must "separate" himself from — everything in our lives of which he is not the Creator, Source, and Guide. This is a terrifying thought; but Jesus forces it upon us.

This is why he concluded his "I say to you" passages in the Sermon on the Mount, which we were just examining, with the words: "You, therefore, *must be perfect,* as your heavenly Father is perfect." (Matt. 5:48.) Notice that the tense here is not the indicative, but rather the imperative ("must")! This is not a suggestion, but a command. He is not holding up an ideal and inviting or encouraging us to strive for it. He is voicing *the demand of the holy God.* To know that God is holy is to know that this demand of perfection, as *he* has defined perfection in Christ, is the only demand that could be voiced in his name.

This is a very uncomfortable acknowledgment. It makes us squirm down inside. This is why we are so slow to make it, and why it has almost disappeared from the popular notions of "religion" in recent years. We would much rather imagine that God is some sort of jovial, indulgent grandfather, and that he surely will be satified if we "do our best." It disturbs us to entertain the possibility that God takes the fact that he is God seriously — even if we do not.

It is precisely this acknowledgment which Jesus forces upon us. He reminds us that God judges (and *must* judge) and separates himself from (and *must* separate himself from) everything in our lives that is not worthy of his presence. He *must* because he is a *holy* God.

2. *The recognition.* When we acknowledge that God is holy, we immediately recognize that there is something radically

wrong at the root of our lives. If we define the word " perfect "
by the life and words of Jesus, and then measure ourselves by
a standard like that, is there *anything* in our lives that is
worthy of the presence and blessing of God? If it is intended
that we should follow the will of God in all things, as Jesus
followed it even in the face of certain death, can we point to
*anything* in our lives wherein we have not intruded our will
upon God's? If completely outgoing, selfless concern is demanded of us in all things, have we fulfilled God's demand in
*anything?*

It is when we have acknowledged that God is holy and find
ourselves forced to ask questions such as these, that we recognize the truth about ourselves *for the first time*. It is then
that we understand what the Bible means by this offensive
little word " sin."

Jesus demands, in the name of God, that we give our lives
selflessly in the service of God. The ungarnished truth is that,
beneath all our pious pretense to the contrary, we spend our
days in the service of ourselves. Since the holy God *demands*
otherwise, this is mutiny against the Almighty. It is *rebellion
against God*.

This is the fabric of sin. " The essence of sin," said Martin
Luther, " is that man seeks his own in everything, even in
God." This is the biography of each of us. We labor unceas-
ingly to turn our vocations, our financial ventures, our social
contacts, our friendships, and every other area of life to our own
good and profit, rather than seek to serve God through them.
We even try to *use* God, seeking " the good life," " integration
of personality," " protection," " peace of mind," " happiness,"
or some other self-chosen and self-centered end through our
religion. Or we seek to " save our souls," or to " get to heaven,"
blandly (or blatantly) ignoring the pointed words of Jesus:
" Whoever would save his life will lose it." (Matt. 16:25.) We

usually are rather subtle and sophisticated in this; but by some manner or means we eventually try to turn virtually everything unto ourselves, even God. This is the very antithesis of what he demands. Thus it is rebellion against God; and rebellion against God is sin.

Kierkegaard insisted that the distinctive mark of modern man is arrogance in the face of God. In his ironic way he remarked that this " has almost tempted God to feel uncertain about himself, like a king who waits anxiously to learn whether the Constitutional Assembly will make him an absolute or a limited monarch."

It might have been more charitable — as well as more accurate — if Kierkegaard had said (as, of course, he does elsewhere, and repeatedly) that this has been, and is the mark of *all* men. Most of us are seldom openly arrogant toward God. But when Jesus has redefined the dimensions of God's will for us, it immediately becomes apparent that hidden arrogance (which sparks rebellion) is our most characteristic response to him. There is, as Paul, Augustine, Luther, and Calvin insisted, a persistent " curved-inness " about our lives, which (only one excepted) *no* man, ancient *or* modern, has escaped.

We also must recognize that this is not merely the truth about the lives of all of us some of the time, and some of us all of the time, but is the truth about all of us all of the time. It is the " watermark " of *all* human life. This is what Paul was confessing when he said that we are " slaves of sin." His point is that sin is not simply an occasional *act;* it also is a persistent *fact.* Jesus implied this when he said that men are " sinners." We not only sin: we are sinners.

This is the recognition that is forced upon us by the life and words of Jesus. Our rebellion against God is an unceasing condition, one that we cannot remember having been free of, and one that no man conquers in himself. The novelist Evelyn

Waugh has characterized man as the creature who harbors "a hot spring of anarchy" within his breast. This is the point. We all are ready and willing to confess that we do stupid and wrong things, things that we should not have done. We also will confess that we ought to do many things that get left undone. The basic problem, however, lies deeper than these "sins," regardless of how serious they may be. Jesus forces us to look beneath these intermittent *acts,* to the *fact* — the tragic fact that our very existence is one of unceasing rebellion against God. We live "bent-in" lives, oriented unto ourselves, when God demands that we live unto him. This is "sin"; and this is our story.

Facing the fact of the holiness of God, and accepting the knowledge of our slavery to sin which comes with facing this fact, is one giant step toward an understanding of Christ. Admittedly, it is not an easy step to take. The alternative of self-deception as we deal with ourselves, and of pretense as we live with our neighbors, always is open to us.

This kind of hoodwinkery we can no longer practice, however, without remembering that Jesus bluntly labeled it "hypocrisy" (which literally means "play acting"). He had a great deal to say about this. It is, in fact, the one thing that he condemned *most* frequently, and *most* scathingly. In so doing he slammed in our faces the door to our last refuge from his great accusation.

In one of his novels, Norman Mailer tells of a Hollywood philosopher, a middle-aged movie actress, whose forte was character analysis. "She had categories," the author explains. "There were good guys, bastards [also a Biblical category; see Deut. 23:2], and phonies, and the worst was a phony. A good guy, I learned by example, was a guy who made no excuses about looking out for himself. A bastard was a man who had

the same philosophy but took extra pleasure in hurting people. A phony was somebody who claimed to be concerned with
anything but himself."

We should notice that the common characteristic shared by
all is "looking out for himself." And we should notice that
those who pretend otherwise are at the very bottom of the
scale. Jesus uses the category "hypocrite," but the point is the
same. His most biting indictments are not of the morally de-
generate, the traitors, prostitutes, adulterers, thieves, and murderers. They are of the "phonies," and particularly of the
"religious" phonies. He brings his most caustic judgment
down upon those who refuse to face the truth about themselves,
and thus live their lives "play acting," pretending that they
are other than what they are.

He once put the *acknowledgment* and the *recognition* that
are demanded of us, if we are to receive and understand his
meaning, in an unforgettable story:

"Two men went up into the temple to pray, one a Pharisee
and the other a tax collector. The Pharisee stood and prayed
thus with himself, 'God, I thank thee that I am not like other
men, extortioners, unjust, adulterers, or even like this tax collector. I fast twice a week, I give tithes of all that I get.' But
the tax collector, standing far off, would not even lift up his
eyes to heaven, but beat his breast, saying, 'God, be merciful
to me a sinner!' I tell you [Jesus added] *this* man went down
to his house justified rather than the other." (Luke 18:9-14.)

And it is only when *we* stand where this man stood ("far
off" from the holy God), and confess what this man confessed ("God, be merciful to me a sinner"), that we have
opened ourselves to the meaning of the cross.

# 3

## THE CROSS

If you are a fast reader, during the time that it takes you to read this chapter someone in the United States will kill himself. If you are a slow reader, two or three persons will commit suicide while you are reading. It happens about every twenty minutes, more than sixty times a day every day. *Why?*

The American Medical Association reports that 19,000,000 sleeping pills are taken every night, just in the United States. This totals about 7,000,000,000 sleeping pills per year. This is 1,000 per cent more than twenty years ago. *Why?*

In addition to mountains of "goof balls," "red devils," "green dragons," "blue heavens," "yellow jackets," and "gee-gee Geronimos," Americans consume about 11,000,000 *pounds* of aspirin each year. This is some 17,000,000,000 aspirin tablets. The use of "tranquilizers" or "tranquillity pills" is increasing so swiftly that any figure printed in a book would be out of date a month later. *Why?*

### Guilt — and the "Sense of Guilt"

There doubtless are many reasons for this situation. The psychiatrists insist that the "sense of guilt" is at the root of much of it. Many of them quarrel with religion because it aggravates our feelings of guilt. This is true, even though it may be only part of the truth. People recognized this "modern" insight long before the twentieth century: "If thou, O Lord, shouldst mark iniquities, Lord, who could stand?" (Ps. 130:3.) Confronted with the holiness of God, men inevitably feel a "sense of guilt." And if religion did nothing more than this, those who insist that it is a blight rather than a blessing would be quite right.

There is a lot of fuzzy thinking today about guilt. It has suddenly become a favorite theme of novelists, playwrights, and poets, and even a popular conversation piece at cocktail parties. But we should notice a very important thing. Quite frequently it is not really guilt that is being discussed, but the "sense of guilt."

A "sense of guilt" ordinarily accompanies guilt, but not necessarily. It is possible to commit a crime, and *be* guilty without *feeling* guilty. The courts encounter this every day. It also is possible to *feel* guilty about something without *being* guilty. The psychiatrists encounter this every day.

Guilt, and a "sense of guilt," are quite different things. We need to make two important distinctions between them.

1. The first is that guilt has reality outside of and apart from our minds, whereas a "sense of guilt" may be quite real, but it is real only in our minds.

For example, if I bash my neighbor on the head because he plays his television set too loudly, and the blow is fatal, I am *guilty* of his death. This adds something objectively real to my life, something outside of my mind and over which I have no control after it comes into existence. Whether I *feel* guilty, or do not feel guilty, is irrelevant to the fact that something has become a part of my life that was not there before: the *guilt* of murdering my neighbor.

2. The second difference between guilt and a "sense of

guilt" is that guilt is permanent and indelible, whereas a "sense of guilt" need not be so. The guilt will always remain; but it is possible for a "sense of guilt" to be dissolved by psychiatric treatment, or to wither away with the passage of time.

Once again, if I murder my TV-playing neighbor, nothing can alter or obliterate this fact and the guilt that accompanies it. I may serve a prison sentence for what I did, pay the widow's grocery bills, send her children to college, and in all sorts of other ways try to "atone" and "make amends." In this way I may ease, or even virtually erase from my mind, my "sense of guilt." But nothing that I can do will wipe out my guilt. This is permanent and indelible.

These distinctions are important because if we are vexed only by the problem of our "sense of guilt," we are avoiding the basic issue, which is guilt itself. Much recent discussion has tended to cloud this fact. Guilt is often discussed as though the psychological and personality problems associated with it were the only problems. Many churches have been swept along in this current. Someone has mused that the churches have become so preoccupied with neurosis and psychosis that many church members probably imagine that they are two Biblical characters, like Aquila and Priscilla.

Neurotic and psychotic guilt feelings, the guilt complex, and the "sense of guilt" all are very real and serious problems. They are, in fact, among our most serious problems in contemporary Western culture. Nevertheless, an encounter with the man Jesus forces us to acknowledge that, as serious as they are, these problems are one step removed from the *most* serious problem, the problem of our guilt itself. This becomes the basic problem for the Christian, and the one with which he must primarily be concerned.

This is true because when we encounter Jesus two things result. He *redefines* our guilt over against the holiness of God, and he *redirects* it to God. Let us examine these two things briefly:

1. Guilt can be defined religiously as the permanent hang over of sin. When Jesus recasts our sense of "oughtness" (as we saw in the previous chapter), he forces us to acknowledge the sin, the state of rebellion, that is hidden beneath the surface of our lives. This reveals a breadth and a depth to our guilt that are staggering. In bringing us to the recognition that we are guilty even for the hidden thoughts and desires in our lives that have violated the will of the holy God, he *redefines* the proportions of our guilt and turns it into a permanent crisis.

This is what threw the Pharisees into a frenzy. They had managed to avoid murder, adultery, drunkenness, perjury, robbery, et cetera, et cetera, and they had congealed into a state of comfortable self-satisfaction as a result. When Jesus opened up the heart of the matter and pointed out that they were nonetheless guilty for every angry thought, every lustful desire, every feeling of jealousy or hatred, et cetera, et cetera, this jolted their self-satisfaction and threw their whole way of life into turmoil. When he had *redefined* their guilt it took on proportions of which they had not even dreamed.

2. Jesus also *redirects* our guilt by revealing, to our utter chagrin, that it is first of all guilt *before God*. When we betray the trust of our employer, offend a friend, or inflict suffering upon our family, we have of course sinned against our employer, our friend, or our family. This in itself is serious enough. But Jesus forces us to recognize that there is something infinitely more serious: the fact that all sin initially is sin against our Creator.

He makes painfully clear what the psalmist meant when he cried out to God, "Against thee, thee only, have I sinned" (Ps. 51:4). This means that every betrayal, every offense.

every infliction of suffering — although our neighbor may be the victim — is first of all sin against God. Here our sin becomes a terrifying problem, because the primal guilt that it creates is *guilt before God*.

What can we do about *this* kind of guilt?

Nothing.

Nothing?

Exactly nothing.

We live in a do-it-yourself age, but here all " self-help techniques " are futile. We cannot solve this problem by taking up a hobby, or going to Florida, or buying a book, or adopting a cause, or thinking positive thoughts. Even psychiatric treatment finds its limits here. Much can be done for exaggerated or misplaced feelings of guilt or for an irrational " sense of guilt." But we can do precisely nothing, and there is precisely nothing that anyone can do for us to rid us of our guilt.

. . . *Unless God himself should do something.*

### The Supreme Enigma

It is here that the cross of Christ enters human experience. When we initially ponder the fact, it is one of the strangest anomalies in all history that the first Christians should have found the cross freeing them from their guilt. How could this be? All that possibly can be said of this event, as historical fact, is: here a peasant carpenter was cruelly nailed to a crude cross. Yet the early church looked back at this brutal execution and saw in it *the supreme instance of the hand of God molding human history, and the final unveiling of the divine love.*

There is not a shred of evidence to suggest that anyone drew these conclusions when this event occurred. At the moment it could only be regarded as tragedy. The Gospels are utterly frank in their admission that the moment of the death of Jesus was one of complete disillusionment for his disciples. Rather than seeing it as " the supreme instance of the hand of God molding human history," they saw it as the defeat of their Master, and by that same token as the defeat of God. Rather than seeing it as " the final unveiling of the divine love," they saw it as brutal, tragic, and even (as one writer has put it) " obscene." The divine love was surely veiled, rather than unveiled, at this point.

This is why it is so utterly astonishing to find these same disciples, as they burned out their lives carrying forward the mission and the message that Jesus had committed to them, looking back to his crucifixion as the highest moment of meaning and triumph in his life. The more we think about it, the more curious and perplexing it gets. And our astonishment doubles when we notice that nowhere in this persistent preoccupation with the death of Jesus is there the slightest trace of a " funeral " atmosphere, of bereavement or morbidity. The New Testament writers looked back upon this hideous event, which from a factual point of view could only be regarded as black and irreparable defeat, in a spirit that actually was one of joy and triumph. And the mood in which the disciples talked of his death was so exultant that they were accused of being drunk, even at nine o'clock in the morning! (Acts 2:13, 15.)

How can we even begin to account for these strange facts? The perplexity that they create begins to lift only as we see what these first Christians saw. At the moment of the crucifixion they faced in its most intensive form what we have called (in Chapter 1) " the optical problem " of Christianity. This is to say, as he was crucified they found it impossible to see beyond the man Jesus, beyond the overbearing fact of the death of the one on whom they had staked everything. When they watched him die, they could see only the death of his cause and of their hope. Tragedy was the only possible conclusion; and the darkness of despair descended upon them.

What dispelled this darkness? It took the light of a resurrection to dispel it. *Beyond* his death they once more knew his presence, just as they had known it *before* his death. And they knew that he could be with them beyond death only if a mighty act of God had raised him from the dead.

Now the darkness lifted. As it lifted they saw the cross in a new light. What formerly had seemed to be defeat and could only be regarded as tragedy, they now recognized as the supreme victory. Seized by the assurance of the resurrection, they now knew that God had been present in this enigmatic event. It was this — *the conviction that the love of God is unconquerable, and that in the cross this love has appeared and acted in a final and decisive way* — which changed their moment of dark defeat into the moment of greatest victory.

This was a strange experience and a strange conclusion that they drew from it. But it was also a compelling conclusion, the most compelling conclusion that has ever seized man. It completely changed the lives of the disciples, and it has continued to change lives for two thousand years. An incident that has been recounted by H. H. Farmer suggests the compulsive power that flows from it:

" Many years ago I was preaching on the love of God; there was in the congregation an old Polish Jew who had been converted to the Christian faith. He came to me afterward and said, ' You have no right to speak about the love of God, until you have seen, as I have seen, the blood of your dearest friends running in the gutters on a gray winter morning.' I asked him later how it was that, having seen such a massacre, he had come to believe in the love of God. The answer he gave in effect was that the Christian gospel first began to lay hold of him because it bade him see God — the love of God — just where he was, just where he could not but always be in his thoughts and memories — in those bloodstained streets on that gray morning. It bade him see the love of God — not somewhere else, but in the midst of just that sort of thing, in the blood and agony of Calvary. He did at least know, he said, that this was a message that grappled with the facts; and then he went on to say something the sense of which I shall always remember though the words I have forgotten. He said, ' As I looked at that man upon the cross, as I heard him pray, " Father, forgive them, for they know not what they do," as I heard him cry in his anguish, " My God, my God, why hast thou forsaken me? " I knew that I was at a point of final crisis and decision in my life; I knew that I must make up my mind once and for all, and either take my stand beside him and share in his undefeated faith in God . . . or else fall finally into a bottomless pit of bitterness, hatred, and unutterable despair.' "

The cross forces *us* to the edge of this same pit, pushing us to a point of crisis and decision where we must leap into faith or fall into despair. It is not always easy for us to see this. Nietzsche has remarked that " modern men, hardened as they are to all Christian terminology, no longer appreciate the horrible extravagance which lay in the formula, ' God on the cross.' " If this is true, it is not necessary that it be true. The disciples not only found God in the cross and appreciated his " horrible extravagance," but had their lives inverted by it. They discovered that in the death of Christ God had revolutionized their notions about him, and that he had completely changed their relationship to him.

And this is what the cross offers us: *a radical revision of our understanding of God's forgiveness and love* and *a new rela-*

*tionship to him.* These made all the difference to the disciples. Let us examine them, for they can make all the difference to us.

## The Love of God

The early Christians discovered through the cross that the forgiveness and love of God are *unconditional*. Of course, the *idea* of divine love and forgiveness was not new to them. It was securely embedded in their scriptures (our Old Testament). It can even be said that this is the heart of the religion of the Old Testament, where it is true to its essential nature. It has received classic expression, for example, in Psalm 103: " The Lord is merciful and gracious, slow to anger and abounding in steadfast love. . . . He does not deal with us according to our sins, nor requite us according to our iniquities. For as the heavens are high above the earth, so great is his steadfast love toward those who fear him." (Ps. 103:8, 10, 11.)

The idea was not new, but its incarnation in history, its appearance and enactment in human life, was *radically* new. Here the love of God has become a *gift,* brought to earth and offered to all, and without conditions. The same holy God who demands perfect obedience has invaded history, to free us from our bondage to sin and guilt, so that in our new freedom we might obey him.

This is the meaning of " grace." It was in the cross that the grace of God appeared and was unveiled in history, as his purpose and our hope. " Grace " is another word for " love," except that it carries the additional meaning that the love is totally *unmerited,* completely *unearned,* and absolutely *undeserved.* It can be called " in-spite-of " love, because it is offered and given *in spite of* the fact that its recipient in no way deserves to be loved with this kind of love. It is a love that gives everything and requires nothing — except that it be received. This is the nature of the love of God, the love that God *is,* as Jesus established and unveiled this love in his life and death.

The classic picture that Jesus painted of this unconditional, forgiving love is found in the Gospel of Luke, ch. 15:11-32. Tradition has taught us to call this story "the parable of the prodigal son." But since to be "prodigal" means to be extravagant and lavish, we would be much more accurate if we called it the parable of the prodigal God.

For the point of the story is one made about God. And the extravagance of the younger son in this story, as he "squandered his property," is as nothing when it is compared to the extravagance of the father as he lavished his compassion and love. This is the point of the story. It is a radical and revolutionary redefinition of the love of God, the redefinition that Jesus made a part of our life with his life and death. The unconditional, free, full, and complete way in which the father welcomed home his sinful and guilty son — in spite of his sin and guilt: this is the heart of the matter, and the message of the cross.

Jesus was, in reality, here illustrating the meaning of his own life and death. We shall see later in this chapter that the story, or the "message," of this love is in itself not enough, and why it is not enough. But even here we should notice, as P. T. Forsyth somewhere has said, that in a sense Jesus left this story incomplete. He had to complete it with his death; and men could not have understood it had he not done so. The cross shows us, as it were, a God who has himself gone into the "far country" where we dwell, into the very fleshpots and swine holes in which we live, to "bring us home." It was this *act* of God in Christ which made it possible for us to believe the unbelievable news of his unconditional love. It is at the cross that we know that this is not news " from afar off." It is " the Word of God " become flesh of our flesh, even unto death, that we might know that his love is unconquerable and *unconditional*.

The crucifixion itself tells us this. As Jesus looked down at those who had just nailed him to the cross, and prayed, " Father, forgive them " (Luke 23:34), he placed no conditions on this forgiveness. He did not demand that his persecutors cease to persecute him. He did not require that they pull out the nails, bind up the wounds, and release him. He did not ask that they do something special to " atone," or to make up for their present or for their past deeds. He did not even demand that they feel regretful for what they had done. He just prayed, " Father, forgive them." He forgave them *as they were*.

This is the unbelievable nature of the forgiveness that God offers *us*. It is without conditions. That is, God does not require (or even request) that we become something that we are not, to make ourselves more worthy of his love. He loves us *as we are,* in spite of what we are. As the love of Christ neither wavered nor waned, even as the nails were driven into his hands and feet, and the spear thrust into his side, so the love of God never wavers and never wanes — whatever we may *do,* whatever we may *be,* or whatever we may *become*. He loves us; and he forgives us — " as is," and in spite of all — because he *is* love.

It is needless to say that this is a kind of love that is not only strange, but completely foreign to us — except as we know it through Christ. *Our* love is something very different. We love those whom we find to be lovable, or whom we admire and enjoy. We are forever trying to change or " improve " those whom we love most, so that they will be more lovable, i.e., so that we can love them more. And we love in the hope and expectation of being loved in return. We find it impossible to love those who are to us unlovable, or whom we do not admire or enjoy. And if our love is spurned or betrayed, we withdraw it, and it dies.

This is why we must say that Jesus radically revises our notion of "love." Luther called this new love which we find in the cross "*lost* love." It is completely different from our calculated, manipulating kind of love. It is unconditional and extravagant, a prodigal love. It is offered freely and without "strings." It is lavished upon the unlovable. It demands nothing in return. It is, Luther said, like a mountain spring that gushes forth. A spring flows neither because of man's need nor because of earth's desire. Nor does it cease to flow when it flows uselessly, when its water wends its way to the sea without being used or appreciated. A spring flows because it is its nature to flow, and it continues to flow because it must.

This is how God loves and forgives us. He loves and forgives, and continues to love and forgive, in spite of all, because — and just because — he *is* love.

## The Cost of Forgiveness

Can we accept this kind of forgiveness and love? In theory, there would appear to be no problem here. We imagine that the real problem is to persuade people (and persuade God) to forgive us and to love us. We also imagine that although this sometimes is difficult, it is not *too* difficult. A character in W. H. Auden's Christmas Oratorio, *For the Time Being,* states it quite baldly: "I like committing crimes. God likes forgiving them. Really, the world is admirably arranged."

Actually the matter is not quite so simple. Theory and life can be quite different, as they certainly are here. The truth is that when we are offered forgiveness under circumstances where we are sharply conscious that we do not deserve it, we find that *accepting forgiveness can be one of the hardest things in the world*. The penetrating French writer, Gabriel Marcel, has written a play that pictures this clearly. Entitled *A Man of God,* it is the story of a minister and his wife, Claude and Edmee Lemoyne.

Early in their married life, Edmee had betrayed her husband. The "other man" in the story is the real father of their teen-age daughter. Claude knew of this affair when it happened. He also knew that his daughter was not really his. Following months of inner agony, his decision had been to offer his wife his complete forgiveness, and he had forgiven her.

In restrospect he says: "Yes, I forgave her. And I shall never forget what that did for me, the inner peace it brought, the sense of a Power working with me and not instead of me, strengthening my will but not supplanting it. Since that day I've seen my way clear."

Claude had imagined through the years that both his and God's forgiveness had been accepted by Edmee, and that the matter was a closed book. When it suddenly is reopened by the appearance of the other man, he discovers that Edmee has been completely unable to accept his forgiveness. Her whole life has been colored by the fact that, although forgiven, she could not accept forgiveness.

Claude's brother, who is a physician, has sensed this. His comment on Edmee's life during these intervening years is a telling description of the "good life" lived by so many — a life outwardly "good," but inwardly burdened by guilt and unable to accept forgiveness and love. Edmee is, the brother says, "so austere, so wrapped up in her duties, so absorbed in good works. It gives me the impression of a sleepwalker. I sometimes feel that your wife is going through life half unconscious."

When the incident is reopened by the reappearance of the other man, Claude reiterates his forgiveness. What else can he do? But when he reminds his wife that he has forgiven her, he is astonished when she replies:

"I'm sick of your tolerance. I'm sick of your broad-mindedness. It nauseates me. What do you expect me to do with all this generosity that cost you nothing?"

"Nothing," he reiterates, "when I *forgave* you?"

Breaking into sobs, she bursts out: "What was your forgiveness for? What do you want me to do with it? *What good is it to me?*"

This is *real* life. It may be very difficult to forgive. That is what Claude discovered. But it may be far harder to accept forgiveness, particularly when we need it most. That is what Edmee discovered. And when we recall our earlier discussion of the way that sin creates guilt, and remember our earlier distinction between guilt and a "sense of guilt," we realize why.

Claude could forgive his wife. But he could do nothing to erase the *guilt* that Edmee had created. This was something over which neither he nor she had any control. This guilt clung to Edmee, and it created a barrier between her and her husband. He could forgive her, and convince her in her mind that he *had* forgiven her. But nothing that he could say or do could break down this barrier of guilt. When we see this, whether in Edmee, or in another person, or in ourselves, we are staring into the eyes of life's most insuperable problem.

Now we can begin to understand why it is not enough for the cross simply to *show* God's forgiveness. Something must be done about our guilt. We need more than to be told about God's love. In the face of our guilt, sheer "broad-mindedness," like Claude's, "generosity that cost . . . nothing," may, as Edmee found, do no more than "nauseate" us. It cannot annul our guilt, and so it only makes us more painfully aware of it. We instinctively know that "forgiveness" that costs nothing is not forgiveness. It is easygoing toleration, and this we despise both in ourselves and in others. And if this is true in our human relations, how much more true is it in our relationship to God? We could not worship a God who took our guilt less seriously than we ourselves take it.

This is why the cross is necessary to us. For at the cross God not only *spoke* the message of forgiveness, but also *enacted* that message. It is his *act* that makes it possible for us to accept the "good news" of forgiving love, the "message" that Christ not only talked about but actually incarnated.

This is what Edmee had been unable to realize. And our task now is to try to show how a recognition of what happened on the cross could have made all the difference to Edmee.

And not only to Edmee.

To us.

For the next few pages are not going to make much sense to the person who is sitting complacently on the side lines, uninvolved in all this (apparently morbid) discussion of sin and guilt. The cross will never seem important to the person who does not feel involved in guilt himself, so that, details apart, his problem is basically the same as Edmee's problem: where can I find a forgiveness that is real?

Your guilt may not be adultery or murder (though it may). It may not be bearing false witness (though it is likely you know that it is, if you are honest). It probably is any number of things — and if you should feel that you are guiltless, then it may be worth pondering the matter for a few more minutes. At the least you can discover that you are unique among all human beings — save one — who have ever lived.

To Edmee, and to us, the cross brings three things, at least, that cannot be found apart from it. These are illustrated in the New Testament with three vivid word pictures that we must now examine: one taken from the institution of slavery, one from the ancient rite of sacrifice, and one from the practice of law in Biblical times.

The words that are used to paint these pictures are some of the most difficult in the Bible for modern readers, because the social and religious practices to which they allude are strange to us. We need to see them in their original setting, so that we may see more clearly what they tell us about the overcoming of our guilt.

### 1. *Christ as the one who "redeems" or buys back*

Edmee felt that *something had to be done* to compensate, or "atone," or "make up," for the wrong she had done. In this she was merely voicing what we all feel as we try to rid ourselves of our guilt. She could not accept the forgiveness that Claude offered her because she took her guilt seriously. It mattered not what he *said* to her — her guilt remained. And until something was *done* about this guilt, what he offered as "forgiveness" could only be accepted as easygoing toleration or nauseating indulgence.

It is in the cross that we find the assurance that everything necessary has been done to wipe out the guilt that clings to us and alienates us from God and from one another. Here we discover that what God offers us is not good-natured indulgence of our sin, but *costly* forgiveness. When we visualize Christ hanging in agony on the cross, *dying for us,* we realize that the cross represents the extent to which God was willing to go to reunite us with him. He has not merely told us that we are forgiven. He has done what had to be *done,* in order for his forgiveness to be forgiveness (and not simply indulgence) and in order for us to accept this forgiveness.

The New Testament uses the word picture of the *freeing of a slave* to portray this for us. We have seen (in Chapter 2) that Paul refers to our human plight as " slavery," and why he does so. We saw there that our problem is not merely that we sometimes do things that can be called " sins." It is that we *are* sinners, or that we are helplessly enslaved by our sin, and hopelessly in bondage to our guilt.

Jesus is portrayed by the New Testament as our " Redeemer " and " Deliverer," rescuing us from this enslavement with his death. These words immediately suggested to the first-century Christians the vivid picture of a slave being set free. The slave could be freed from his bondage, but a " ransom " was demanded to do so. The ransom was the price that had to be paid to " reedem " him, or to buy back his freedom.

When these words " Redeemer," " Deliverer," " ransom," " price," and " redemption " appear in the New Testament, they should bring this picture to our minds. Christ came, we are told, " to give his life as a ransom for many " (Mark 10:45). And Paul says, " You are bought with a price." (I Cor. 6:20 and ch. 7:23.) If we can visualize what it meant to a slave to be freed, we know what this is intended to tell us. We know that with his death (the giving of his life) Christ has set us free. He has " paid the price." He has " redeemed " us from our slavery to sin and bondage to guilt.

This is what Edmee did not realize. She felt (as we all feel apart from the cross) that there was something that *she* had to do, some price that *she* had to pay, to atone for her past and wipe out her guilt. And until this price was paid, whatever it might be, she could accept neither the forgiveness of her husband nor the forgiveness of God.

In the cross we discover that everything necessary to our forgiveness has been done. As amazing as it sounds, this means that it is unnecessary for *us* to do anything — because every-thing has been done *for* us. The "price" of our forgiveness and freedom, which was the greatest price possible — the life of the Son of God — has been paid. "In him we have *redemption* through his blood, the forgiveness of our trespasses," Paul says. (Eph. 1:7.) It is the mystery of our faith that when we look at the cross we *know* that our bondage to sin and guilt is broken. We are *set free* for a new life of joyous obedience to God, because with his death Christ has "redeemed" us.

We will, to be sure, try now to do all that we can to set right what was set wrong (though often it is too late for this). But now we will do this, not as a condition of *being* forgiven, but in gratitude for the fact that we *are* forgiven. And between those two there is all the difference in the world.

## 2. Christ as a "sacrifice" for us

Edmee had unconsciously discovered that *God* must do what has to be done in order for her to accept forgiveness. She had made every attempt to "satisfy" the conditions of forgive-ness. She had literally devoted her life to the project of aton-ing, or making amends, for her past. She was "wrapped up in her duties," and could even be described as "absorbed in good works." This apparently had somewhat alleviated the vividness of her "sense of guilt" (at least she seemed "half unconscious"); but it had failed miserably to produce the *costly* forgiveness that she felt was necessary.

What Edmee needed is what the cross offers. It is in the cross that we discover that *God* has done what must be done to reconcile us to him. The New Testament suggests this by referring to the *Old Testament practice of sacrifice.* The early Christians (who were all Jews) were familiar with the princi-ple of this rite, from Lev. 17:11: "The life of the flesh is in the blood; and I have given it for you upon the altar to make atonement for your souls; for it is the blood that makes atonement, by reason of the life."

Here it is recognized that because of the gravity of his sin, man deserves only judgment and death from God. The great prophets had deepened the sense of this fact. This is why it was felt that the sacrifice of *life* and nothing less than life was required for forgiveness. It was this feeling which underlay the seriousness with which the sacrificial system was regarded in later Judaism.

The New Testament uses the word picture of this rite to suggest the meaning of the death of Christ. His death is referred to as a " sacrifice," or as an " expiation "; and, in reference to one of the animals sacrificed, he is called " the Lamb of God, who takes away the sin of the world." In conformity with the Old Testament view stated above — that life resides in the blood — there are frequent references in the New Testament to " the blood of Christ," to the " shed blood " of his " broken body," and to " the blood of the Lamb." These are intended to suggest that it is the sacrifice of his life that procures our forgiveness when on our own merits we deserve nothing but death.

In all of this, the New Testament writers wish to call before our minds the picture of the ancient practice of sacrifice. We should notice that by the ancient principle it was *God* who gave the " life " to be sacrificed (" *I* have given it for you . . . to make atonement."). This emphasis is continued when the New Testament uses this picture. Jesus is " the Lamb of *God*." " All this is *from God*," Paul reminds us. (II. Cor. 5:18.) And again, " He . . . did not spare his own Son, but gave him up for us all." (Rom. 8:32.) This is a first principle: it is *God* who has " provided the sacrifice," which is to say that it is *God* who has done what had to be done to forgive our sin and annul our guilt.

Edmee had finally recognized, after years of attempting to do so with her " good works," that there was nothing that she could do to "atone" for her past. When we, with Edmee, finally realize this, we know that if anything is to be done, *God* must do it. And when we finally come to this realization, the word picture taken from the ancient rite of sacrifice says something crucial to us.

It tells us that *God* has provided the necessary "sacrifice" and "satisfaction" for us, that he has "given up" his Son, even unto death, for our forgiveness. The perplexity of our lives is that so often we cannot accept forgiveness, even when we know that we are forgiven. The mystery of our faith is that when we accept what Christ has done for us on the cross, we *then* can accept the forgiveness that God offers — and in turn can forgive, and accept the forgiveness of, others. We can because, as we look at the cross, we recognize that our forgiveness was *this* costly to God; and because we recognize that *God has himself done what must be done*. In giving his Son to die for us, he has made it possible for us to accept his forgiveness and his love.

### 3. *Christ as the one who " takes our place"*

Edmee was unable to believe the God could forgive *her*. She had no illusions about herself. She knew full well the gravity of what she had done, and she condemned herself for it. She had tried to change herself, to make herself the kind of person whom God could accept; but this in no way altered her past. She knew that if she were to receive what she deserved from God, it could not possibly be forgiveness and love.

It is in the cross that we discover that God *can* accept us, notwithstanding what we have done, and in spite of what we are, because Christ has taken our place. The New Testament uses the word picture of the *practice of law* to illustrate this. It pictures Christ standing in our place before the bar of justice, or before the judge — the holy God. He stands where we should stand, and takes upon himself our rightful judgment. This allows us to receive the judgment that is due to him.

Sometimes when this picture is used, the emphasis is upon the fact that Christ has taken our place and accepted what *we* deserve. In dying for us, he took upon himself the " curse " that our rebellion against God has rightfully brought upon us. He has " become a curse *for us* "; or he was " made sin *for us* " (Gal. 3:13 and II Cor. 5:21). This would bring to the mind of the early Christians the well-known picture in Isa., ch. 53: " The Lord has laid on him the iniquity of us all." When he hung upon the cross he took *our* place, taking upon himself our judgment and condemnation.

At other times when this picture is used, the emphasis is upon our receiving what *he* deserves. He stands before the judge " in our stead," so that we might receive the sentence that *his* life merits. The judge pronounces upon us the judgment that *he* deserves, rather than the judgment that we deserve, because he has taken our place.

Paul is suggesting this picture when he says that if we are " in Christ," God " justifies the *un*godly." He does so not because he is tricked, or because we have in some way made ourselves " godly," but because our life is " hid with Christ in God." Paul repeats again and again that we are " justified," and that this " justification " is the door to new life. The word is a legal term, which, when it is used in this word picture, means that we are pronounced righteous by the judge — even though we are *not* righteous — because Christ has taken our place at the bar of judgment. Thus we find ourselves in a new relationship to God, an astounding *guilt-free* relationship, because " one man's act of righteousness leads to acquittal and life for all men " (Rom. 5:18).

We all are one with Edmee in that in our deeper selves we know that we do not deserve the forgiveness and love of God. Nor will we ever merit his blessing. Even if we could cease to be what we *are* (which, of ourselves, we cannot), we can do nothing about what we *have been*. This is why we are (rightfully) sure that a holy God cannot accept us, and that we deserve only his wrath and judgment.

But when we turn away from ourselves, to the cross, we discover — to our utter amazement — that we *are* forgiven in spite of all, because of what Christ has done for us. In taking upon himself what we deserve, the unconditional judgment of God upon our sin, he made it possible for us to receive what he deserves, the unconditional love of God. It is the cross that makes it possible for us to accept this forgiveness and love of which we are, and know that we are, completely unworthy.

It is in this acceptance that we discover that the " bruises " and " wounds " of Christ were for our healing, and that they heal our broken, shattered lives. When we accept his death, recognizing that he died to redeem us from our sin and guilt, we find that we have accepted a *new life* — the new life of grateful and joyous obedience to God, which is possible only as the forgiveness and love of God become " our daily bread."

## The Fundamental Fact of Our Faith

These New Testament word pictures do not " explain " the meaning of the cross. The cross, beyond all else, can be " understood " only as we " stand under " it, or only as — and in so far as — it becomes an ever-present reality in our deepest experience. But these pictures, and the key words with which they are painted, are essential because they keep before us the fundamental fact of our faith: that Christ died for our sins.

It is important to notice that this *is* a " fact." It is something that *has happened*. It does not need our faith in it to be true, or our understanding of it to be actual. It is a " finished work."

This means that our faith is founded upon an actuality, not upon a possibility. It rests upon something that has actually happened, not upon something that might possibly happen. " God has prepared reconciliation for us even before we entered the struggle against him," remarks Karl Barth. We do not live in the wistful hope that he *will* reconcile and forgive us. We live under the deep assurance that he *has* reconciled and forgiven us.

This is the most tremendous realization that can seize us in life. It is what gives a granite-like foundation to Christian living. When we take our stand under the cross, we are not asked to build upon the shaky foundation of our " feeling " about God, or our " experience " of God, or even our " faith " in God. These, at best, will always be uncertain and confused. And we are not asked to build upon some supposed " goodness " in our lives, or some " good works " that we may have done or might do. We can never be sure that we do not help others to help ourselves. We cannot even be sure that our service to God is not a disguised self-service.

But the Christian life is founded upon none of these. Its foundation was constructed when God acted in the cross. Thus we need not grope for a possibility. We can take our stand upon an actuality. " God was in Christ, reconciling the world to himself," Paul says. (II Cor. 5:19.) God *has* forgiven and reconciled us: herein lies the stability of our faith. It is the stability of this act, this fact.

And because this *is* the fact upon which our faith is founded, it obviously *should be* the fact upon which we found our faith.

# 4

## THE INCARNATION

Mahatma Gandhi, the famous Indian leader, once said: "I have never been interested in a historical Jesus. I should not care if it were proved by someone that the man called Jesus never lived, and that what was narrated in the Gospels were a figment of the writer's imagination. For the Sermon on the Mount would still be true for me."

Gandhi was a great man; but, by any significant definition of the word, he was not (as he himself recognized) a " Christian." His kind of approach to Christianity might be possible except for the fact that Jesus himself makes it impossible. Not only in the Sermon on the Mount, but throughout all his teaching, he frames the issue in such a way that the question of *who he was and is* cannot be avoided.

He does not ask us simply to accept his teaching, but to accept *him* — even in the famous Sermon on the Mount, which is usually, as in the case of Gandhi, the pretext for claiming that *who he is* is unimportant. " Blessed are you," he says, " when men revile you and persecute you and utter all kinds of evil against you falsely *on my account*." (Matt. 5:11.) He even pictures himself as the judge on the Day of Judgment, standing at the gate of heaven allowing only those who can pass *his* judgment to " enter the kingdom." He says: " On that day many will say to me, 'Lord, Lord, did we not prophesy in your name, and cast out demons in your name, and do many mighty works in your name?' And then will I declare to them, 'I never knew you; depart from me, you evildoers.'" (Matt. 7:22-23.)

## The Issue

Familiarity tends to blunt the edge of the surprise (or the shock) that we ought to feel when we are confronted by the claims that Jesus made, and that have been made about him. They are of such magnitude that a French scholar could en- title a book *The Insanity of Jesus;* and the issue actually *is* this clear-cut when we face it candidly.

This is why the question of *incarnation* cannot be avoided. This technical term is built on the Latin word for " flesh," and literally means "enfleshment." Was this man the " enflesh- ment" of God? A familiar Christmas carol ("Hark! the Herald Angels Sing") calls him " the Incarnate Deity." The familiar Christmas word "Emmanuel" means "God with us." Was this man, in some mysterious way, God appearing in human flesh?

Consider:

He repeatedly forgave sins, not in the name of God, but by his own authority. He said to the paralytic, " Your sins are forgiven." (Matt. 9:2.)

He proclaimed that with his appearance the prophecies of the Old Testament were fulfilled. " Today this scripture has been fulfilled in your hearing." (Luke 4:21.)

He announced that with his ministry the reign of God had arrived. "If it is by the Spirit of God that I cast out demons, then the kingdom of God has come upon you." (Matt. 12:28.)

He accepted the confession that he was " the Messiah," that he was " sent " by God. When Peter said, "You are the

Christ," he replied, " Blessed are you." (Matt. 16:16-17.)

He said, in what is perhaps the most " offensive " (i.e., offense-giving) statement of all, " All things have been delivered to me by my Father; and no one knows the Son except the Father, and no one knows the Father except the Son and any one to whom the Son chooses to reveal him." (Matt. 11:27.)

He also said, " Blessed is he who takes no offense at me." (Matt. 11:6.)

So run the accounts in Matthew and Luke. The Fourth Gospel put it even more bluntly. Here Jesus says: " *I am* the way, and the truth, and the life; no one comes to the Father, but *by me.* . . . I am *in* the Father and the Father *in me.* The words that I say to you I do not speak on my own authority; but the Father *who dwells in me* does his works." " *I and the Father are one.*" (John: 14:6, 10 and ch. 10:30.)

The popular British writer, C. S. Lewis, has addressed one of his provocative little books, *The Case for Christianity,* to this issue. His purpose, he says, is " to prevent anyone from saying the really silly thing that people often say about Him: ' I'm ready to accept Jesus as a great moral teacher, but I don't accept his claim to be God.' "

With all the delicacy of a battering ram, Lewis continues: " That's the one thing we mustn't say. A man who was merely a man and said the sort of things Jesus said wouldn't be a great moral teacher. He'd either be a lunatic — on a level with the man who says he's a poached egg — or else he'd be the devil of hell. You must make your choice. Either this man was, and is, the Son of God: or else a madman or something worse. You can shut him up for a fool, you can spit at him and kill him as a demon; or you can fall at his feet and call him Lord and God. But don't let us come with any patronizing nonsense about his being a great human teacher. He hasn't left that open to us. He didn't intend to." This is the issue.

It is the issue that Jesus forced with his life, his death, and his words; and it cannot be watered down. Who *was* this man who forgave sins? . . . who insisted that the prophecies of the ages were fulfilled in him? . . . who announced that with his coming the reign of God had come? . . . who accepted the confession that he was "sent" by God? . . . who insisted that God can be known only through him?

Was he lunatic? . . . devil? . . . madman? . . . or the incarnation of God? What must we say of a man in whom millions have found the very holiness and love of God, who has continued to make his presence known beyond death, and through whom countless multitudes on every part of the globe have found forgiveness of their sin and guilt?

### Creeds, Their Value and Limits

The church hammered out its answer to these questions in the early centuries, in what were called "creeds." (See, for example, the Nicene Creed at the end of this chapter.) The word "creed" is simply our "Englishing" of the Latin word with which such statements of faith began, the word *credo* meaning "I believe."

It is a matter of no small moment that the creeds were formulated under the pressure of "heresies." Heresy is "false belief," but ordinarily it is not falsity as such. It is, rather, truth that has been carried to false extremes. The great heresies *were* great, and were obviously well intentioned. And many of the men whom the church has declared to be "heretics" have been great Christians as well as its outstanding leaders and thinkers.

These observations suggest that heresy should always be respected, even when it must be denied. And it should, both because of the truth that it embraces, and because of the invaluable service that it renders in forcing the church to recover and clarify its faith. In one, very matter-of-fact sense, it was the great heretics who gave us the great creeds.

In the early centuries many teachings were being advanced and championed that threatened the meaning that the church had found in Christ. It was necessary for the church to clarify its common mind on these " false " answers. The replies that it made to these heresies are what we know as the " creeds " of the early Christian church, such as the Nicene Creed, the Athanasian Creed, and others. Some people today are inclined to dismiss these creeds out of hand, as outworn relics of the past. Other people still find them the most adequate means available for stating their own faith. We should do neither without giving a great deal of thought to the matter.

The attitude that we have toward these early creeds should take into account both the time and the circumstances of their origin. To do so is to gain both a positive and a negative factor. The *positive* factor is this: a reminder that a creed is not a matter of private opinion, or as we say, " one man's opinion " (". . . and I am entitled to mine "). On the contrary, a creed is *the church articulating its faith*. It is obvious that no individual could speak, or can speak, for the church. But the church must speak its common mind, and in its historic creeds and confessions this is precisely what it has tried to do.

The creeds do not carry the authority of God. They are not divine utterances. But they *do* carry the authority of the church. They were written by the church and for the church. They can be discarded, altered, or replaced, as they often have been. But this also must be done by the church. We can quibble with them, dispute them, or ignore them, as we often do. But we should not do so except with the greatest care and concern, because they are the voice of the church echoing down the halls of our heritage, giving form to the faith within which men have conquered life and death.

But we spoke also of a *negative* factor. It is this: creeds are always fallible human products, and should be regarded as such. No human statement can express the fullness of the meaning of God for human life. At its best it will always be no more than a stammering, fragmentary attempt to do what can never be done. In this sense the creeds of Christendom are monuments to the church's failures to express what it must always try to express, but can never fully express.

This is why John Calvin insisted that "creeds should be sung." What he meant was that creeds are not so much precise theological formulations that encompass the totality of the faith, as they are corporate acts of praise and adoration on the part of the Christian community, for which the proper mode of expression is joyful and grateful song. When anyone thinks that he has encompassed God in a human statement, we can be sure that it is only a creature of his own invention that he has succeeded in snaring. The great creeds make no such claims, and we should not make them in the name of the creeds.

These comments, then, should indicate a two-sided attitude that we need to bring to the creedal statements about Christ. Paul called Christ God's "*inexpressible* gift," which certainly underlines the fact that no creed has captured and exhausted, or ever can capture and exhaust, the meaning of Christ; nor can all the creeds of all the centuries laid end to end.

Nevertheless, we are not allowed by this fact simply to remain silent. We can only communicate our faith in Christ by stating what that faith is, however inadequate may be the way we state it. The creeds have been Christendom's attempt to do just that. They are the definitive, authoritative statements that the church has made about its faith in Christ.

Luther once said that when we attempt to express the meaning of Christ " we are like little children learning to speak, who can speak only in half words or quarter words." The " half words " and " quarter words " that comprise the creeds of the church are the voice of the church speaking to itself, and to its members individually, describing its faith in Christ. They must stand; and we should stand under them, except as the church speaks more clearly. Yet we should do so, fully recognizing that at best they are poor human " half words or quarter words."

### Heresies, Old and New

We have seen that creeds are the attempt of the church to state its faith. But we must now examine in more detail the fact (alluded to briefly above) that the creeds were also attempts to make clear what the church did *not* believe, to exclude certain points of view that, when pressed, had disastrous consequences. Someone has put the point in extreme but telling form by saying that the creeds are more important for what they refuse to say than for what they say, or for what they *ex*clude than for what they *in*clude.

This is why the great fourth-century church father, Athanasius, referred to the creeds that define the meaning of Christ as " signposts against heresy." They were written against heresy, to be used against heresy (by *us* against the heresy *in us* as well as by the church against " heretics "). They cannot create Christian faith *in* us; but, as " signposts," they can and do mark its outer boundaries *for* us.

The fact that the creeds were framed to speak to *specific* heresies both determines their nature and content, and limits their usefulness today. When a ship is listing dangerously, it can be saved only by shifting the weight to the other side. This is the story of the creeds. They picture for us the church shifting the weight of meaning, placing it where it was needed in the teeth of the immediate storm that threatened.

This makes it all the more important that we recognize, and be able to identify, the "heresies" that threaten the essential meaning that is unveiled for us in the life, death, and resurrection of Christ. What the church has said in the past was in large part determined by what *needed* to be said at a particular time. In the same way, what we need to say to ourselves today about the meaning of Christ is in large part determined by the heresies that threaten our faith. This means that we must be able to spot our heresies.

There are three classic types of Christological heresy, which, broadly speaking, were the three heresies over against which the church framed its creedal statements about the meaning of Christ. And, somewhat to our surprise, we discover that these are very much the same kinds of misunderstandings into which we fall in our own attempts to understand Christ. Therefore, it will be well worth our time to look at each of these in turn.

### 1. *A Manlike God* (*but not* really *a man*)

Before you read farther, answer these questions:

*Do you think that Jesus was ever really tempted to go against the will of God?* (*Yes. No.*)

*Do you think that he knew early in his ministry that he was going to be crucified?* (*Yes. No.*)

*Do you think that he believed that the earth was flat?* (*Yes. No.*)

One temptation that always threatens serious and sincere faith in Christ is the temptation to forget that he was *completely* human. Flakes of this kind of thinking can be found almost everywhere in the church today. Sometimes we worship

Jesus as though he were God, almost forgetting that there is a God. Frequently the doctrine of the Trinity is interpreted in such a way that Jesus becomes a second god (when, as we saw in Chapter 1, the *first* conviction of Christianity has always been that there is one, and only one, God).

The more common guise in which this difficulty appears, however, is the deceptive cloak of a " sacred " vocabulary. We constantly are tempted to wrap Jesus in a cloak of sacred words. We then intimate, or even insist, that those who do not use the particular words and phrases that we use about him do not really " believe " in him (or have not really made a " decision for Christ "). We refuse to look, or allow anyone else to look, behind our words, because we cannot acknowledge that this man *was* in every sense *a man*.

Sometimes the ways in which we refuse to grant that Jesus was completely human are more or less unconscious. If we hesitate, or are unable, to concede that he *really* was tempted, then we are saying that he was not fully human. If we imagine that he was free of the limitations under which we live, such as being bound by space and time, we are denying that he shared fully in our humanity. This is what we are doing when we assume that he had some kind of clairvoyance or omniscience — as, for example, when we assume that he knew early in his life that he would be crucified; or when we suppose that he knew that the world was round, although everyone else in his century believed that it was flat.

It helps to clarify our thinking when we know that there is nothing new about any of this. Each of these well-intentioned, but misguided notions is part of an ancient heresy that the church confronted when it was still in its infancy, and that it has been battling since. A fifth-century bishop (Cyril of Alexandria) accounted for the limitations of the knowledge of Jesus by insisting that " for the profit of his hearers he *pre-*

*tended* not to know." Others, who were called "Seemists," insisted that he only *seemed* to be completely human. He only *seemed* to be hungry and thirsty. He only *seemed* to be tempted. He only *seemed* to suffer and to die. They contended that he could not have been *truly* hungry or thirsty, that he could not *really* have been tempted, that he could not *actually* have suffered and died — because he was God. For them, although he *seemed* to be a man, in reality he was God. He was God appearing in human history in disguise, or God wearing the mask of human nature. He was manlike; but he was a manlike God (and not *really* man).

The church flatly repudiated all of this very early. Against every suggestion that Jesus was a manlike God (and not *really* man), the church insisted that he was "*flesh*," that he was "*very* man" (their word was *vere*, which means truly, really, or actually). When it spoke officially in the creeds, it said that he was "complete in manhood," "of one substance with us as regards his manhood; like us in all respects, apart from sin" (the Council of Chalcedon, A.D. 451).

It is interesting that the very earliest full creed, and the one with which we are most familiar, the so-called Apostles' Creed, shifts the weight of meaning to this side. It emphasizes the *real* human nature of Jesus, that he did not merely "seem" to suffer and die, but actually (and notice how concrete the verbs are) "*suffered* under Pontius Pilate, was *crucified, dead,* and *buried.*"

These early creedal affirmations are crystal-clear. They reveal that the church was determined from the first to allow no shading of the fact of the *real* human nature of Jesus, of his *complete* manhood. The early fathers would not countenance even an implicit suggestion that during his life he was a play-acting god, a divine being merely pretending to be one with us. They insisted uncompromisingly that he was *fully human, veritable man.*

## 2. *A Godlike Man* (*but not* really *God*)

*Which do you think is more important:* (a) *recognizing that Jesus was more than a teacher, or* (b) *living by his teachings?*

*Which more nearly expresses your belief about him:* (a) *he was " a Godly man," or* (b) *he was " God and man "?*

A second possibility is to regard Jesus as a Godlike man, or a very Godly man. One way of doing this is to look upon him primarily as the world's greatest moral example. In recent years it has been a badge of piety to praise him as " a good man," " a very good man," " a very, very good man," " a great man," " the best man who has ever lived," " a remarkable religious personality," or " the perfect example for us."

Another way is to shift the focus of attention to his " teachings." A recent syndicated editorial on the church page of a newspaper, after extolling the need to familiarize our children with " the great moral teachings of our heritage," remarked, " Imagine a school without a picture of Moses, or of Socrates, or of Jesus, or of John Dewey."

When the emphasis is thus placed primarily upon his teachings, Jesus more or less becomes to religion what Euclid was to mathematics. He was the sage of sages, " the wisest man who has ever lived " (probably wiser, even, than Socrates and John Dewey). He saw the truth about God, victorious living, and real peace of mind more clearly, and expressed it more lucidly than it had before (or has since) been seen or expressed.

All of this may be quite true in its own way and place; but what we need to notice is that it does not even raise the Christian issue. Here Jesus remains on the same level with us, even if he is several paces farther along. He is, in one sense or another, merely a Godlike man (and not *really* God); and the issue that the creeds of Christendom force has been completely bypassed.

These are modern forms of an ancient heresy, again one that the church confronted very early. It arose in the beginning because of the numbers among the early Christians who were sensitive to the plural gods of pagan religions, and who were concerned above all to hold to the unity of the one God. This was the normal tendency of many of the Jews in the early church. Every suggestion of a second god was abhorrent and blasphemous to them. Thus when they encountered the tendency of heresy No. 1 — regarding Jesus as a manlike God (and not *really* man), they countered with the questionable corrective of heresy No. 2 — picturing him as a Godlike man (and not *really* God). He was for them " the true prophet "; or he was a man who achieved such goodness and greatness in his life that God " adopted " him as his Son.

Those who interpreted the meaning of Christ in this way emphasized particularly his human struggles and victories as examples that all men should seek to emulate. And they put primary emphasis upon his teachings as " the way " that we should follow. They could not have wedged him between Socrates and Dewey, but the basic emphasis was the same.

Some were so impressed with the holiness of God that it was inconceivable to them that God could himself approach man. They could not bring themselves to call him " Father "; and they even avoided speaking of his " love." Thus they pictured Jesus as a sort of intermediate being, neither really God nor really man, but something between. In this way they could affirm that he was more than man, but without affirming that he was " one " with the Father. He was neither fully human, nor fully divine, but a Godlike man.

It was to this kind of thinking that the church was speaking in its creeds when it insisted that although Jesus was " very man," he also was " God of God," " *Very* God of *Very* God " (the Nicene Creed). At the Council of Chalcedon the official position that the church adopted on the question, against the various heresies that were picturing Jesus as a Godlike man, stated that he was " complete in Godhead," " of one substance with the Father." We shall ask below what the church meant by this; but we should notice here that this bluntly rules out every attempt to exhaust the meaning of Jesus in lavish praise of his teachings, or in pious statements about what a " great man " and " great moral example " he was.

### 3. *God/Man* (*but neither* really *God nor* really *man*)

*When we say that Jesus was " Very God and very man," does this mean that although he " became flesh" he thought the thoughts of God? (Yes. No.)*

*Do you think that the " soul" of Jesus died as well as his body when he was crucified? (Yes. No.)*

When the church insisted that Jesus, although fully human (against heresy No. 1), was " Very God of Very God " (against heresy No. 2), it was inevitable that someone would venture a logical explanation of how this could be true. The attempts that were made were of a piece with our frequent passion to-day for a " logical " or " down-to-earth creed," or for a " common-sense religion " or a " simple gospel."

When we carry this consuming concern for " common sense " to the question of the meaning of Christ, we feel a compulsion to try to explain *how* he could have been both divine and human. Sometimes the suggestion is that he lived a divine life in a human body. Or we may insist that his " soul," or " spirit," or " mind " (or all three) was divine, although his body was like ours.

These also are very old suggestions. The original attempts to explain the incarnation were extremely subtle; but they inevitably suggested, in some manner, that Jesus was divided

within himself, that he was God/man (but neither *really* God
nor *really* man). Some said that the biological side of his
life (the life of the body) was human, but that the spirit that
inhabited this body was divine. They insisted that this did
not mean that he was divided, because his (active) spirit was
united with and controlled his (passive) body. The unavoid-
able implication was, however, that in some sense he was
divided within himself. He was neither *fully* God, nor *fully*
man, but somehow was both mixed up together.

Perhaps these ancient (and our modern) attempts to explain the perplexing questions that are raised by the creeds
serve us best indirectly. They can function as a reminder that
" simple," " logical," " down-to-earth " answers to all our
curious questions are neither possible nor necessary.

This cannot mean, however, that we should cease to ask
these questions. God created us as rational beings; and religion that scorns this fact, and delights in " turning out the
lights," rightfully commands little respect from intelligent
people. When the Creator gave us minds, he must have intended that we should use them, and that we should use them
above all in grasping the truth that he discloses to us. Charles
Williams was right: " Man was intended to argue with God."

It nevertheless is quite another matter to demand arbi-
trarily that God only communicate himself to us in " common-
sense " terms. This can be, in reality, a subtle but nonetheless
arrogant denial of the inescapable element of mystery in
Christian faith. The church always has confessed this element
of mystery and has recognized that it was supremely present
in Jesus Christ. If this be true, it inevitably will be present in
our faith in him and our beliefs about him. This means, as
Karl Barth has bluntly expressed it, that those who talk about
the simple meaning of Christ are simply talking about something else.

This is why the church always has been squeamish about attempts to psychoanalyze Jesus, or to " simplify " him by an identification of what in him was divine and what human. The framers of the early creeds pointedly refused to be lured into this temptation, and in grateful awe they affirmed the mystery that he is " Very God and very man."

## . . . Very Man

We have seen that the traditional confession of the Christian church is *not* that Jesus was a manlike God; or that he was a Godlike man; or even that he was a God/man. It is, rather, that he was and is " Very God and very man." With all its perplexities and difficulties, when we view this affirmation in the light of what the early Christians found in his life, death, and resurrection, we can recognize why they were led to this confession, and why the church has clung to it so tenaciously.

We can also see, when *we* approach as they did (by moving back to it through the meaning that is given to us in the resurrection, death, and life of Jesus) why this is the confession that Christians *must* make about him.

The question of the full, true human nature of Jesus could not (and did not) arise as a serious question for those who shared his life and his ministry. Medieval artists could picture the baby Jesus in the manger as a little adult. But his family and friends *knew* that he was a child, and that he was a teenager, before he became a mature adult. It did not occur to them to question whether it had been necessary for him to grow and mature. They had shared his years of growth and maturity. It is interesting, and informative, that the only chapter in the Gospels about these early years twice makes the statement that he " developed " or " grew." (Luke 2:40, 52.)

Nor did it occur to those who knew him during his life to question the reality of his temptations, his sorrow, his need to eat, sleep, and pray, his pain or his death. (At one point he himself reveals that he had been accused of being a " glutton " and a " drunkard," an accusation that — although obviously in-accurate — probably was not plucked out of thin air. Matt. 11:19.) They knew that his life and his death were completely real because they shared in them.

In addition to the facts of the story, there are recurring testi-monies to this side of the creed throughout the new Testa-ment. " He . . . emptied himself, taking the form of a servant, being born in the likeness of men," Paul says. (Phil. 2:7.) " He *had* to be made like his brethren *in every respect,*" says The Letter to the Hebrews, " so that he might become a merciful and faithful high priest in the service of God, to make expia-tion for the sins of the people." (Ch. 2:17.)

The expression that most accurately records this complete seriousness of the early Christians in the recognition and con-fession that Jesus was " very man " is the phrase " sinful flesh." This was the strongest expression that was available; and there is a mild shock in the fact that they would apply it to one whom they had come to regard as the Messiah and the Son of God — but they *did,* without apology or hesitation. " Sending his own Son in the likeness of sinful flesh and for sin," Paul says, " he [God] condemned sin in the flesh." (Rom. 8:3.)

The temptation to compromise this side of the creed came very early. But there is no indication in the New Testament that the question even occurred to the disciples during his life, and there is every indication that the earliest Christians would have no part of any such compromise. They *knew* that he was " *very* man."

This also is true of us, when without preconceived notions to the contrary we read the record of his life that they have passed on to us. As we watch his struggles and temptations, his agonizing decisions and deep disappointments; as we recognize his hunger and weariness, and see him weep over his people; and when we feel his suffering and pain as he dies upon the cross, what *can* we say . . . except that this man was " *very man* "?

## Very God . . .

Why, then, were the early Christians, and the church officially, led to confess that Jesus was more than man?

We saw in the previous chapter that the full meaning of the cross was not recognized until the light of the resurrection had been shed upon it. In the same manner, it was only as the light of the resurrection was thrown over the death and the life of Jesus that men recognized that *in this man God himself had invaded history and been present with them.*

It was because they found in his continued presence the holy love of God, the holy love that God *is,* that men were led to this confession. This is why they had to say that, although this man was " very man," he also was " *Very God.*" It was for the same reason that the church adopted this as its official creed, its definitive statement about the incarnation. And it is for this selfsame reason that Christians today stand under this affirmation, confessing with the ancient church and Christians of all time, that Jesus was and is " Very God and very man."

When we move back to the question of the incarnation through the resurrection and crucifixion; or when we view the man Jesus whom we see in the Gospels in the light of our personal knowledge of the living Jesus Christ, the knowledge that is ours in the unconditional love and forgiveness that we know as we worship God through him, the temptation to regard the matter as a puzzle or (in Calvin's phrase) " a problem in alchemy " fades into the background. When we do succeed in approaching in this manner, we do not come with preconceived notions of what God *must* be and do, and then attempt to fit Jesus into the little pigeonholes of our private ideas.

We come, rather, in response to his invitation to seek God through him; and we worship in his church, in his name, and under his promises. Then we recognize with the apostles and early Christians that *this* holiness, and *this* love which we find in him, which can convict us as only God can convict us, and yet establish us in an unconquerable assurance of the forgiveness of our sin and guilt . . . this *is* God.

This is why we are prompted to confess that this man is not only " very man " but also " Very God." Luther once said, with almost sublime simplicity, " We find the heart and the will of the Father in Christ." The words that the early councils used to express this conviction were hardly this simple; but they point in the same way to the *crux* of the matter (*crux* is Latin for " cross ").

The Council of Chalcedon affirmed that " our Lord Jesus Christ " is " of one substance with the Father as regards his Godhead, and at the same time of one substance with us as regards his manhood." The word " substance," as it is used here, does not mean " stuff," as we are inclined to understand it. In fact, it meant virtually the opposite when it was written into this creedal statement. The " substance " of something was its " essence," or what makes it what it is — apart from its varying appearances to us.

Thus when the ancient church said that he was " Very God," they were affirming that they had found in the man Christ Jesus the " essence " of God, what makes God " God." They had found in him " the heart and the will of the Father," the very holy love which God *is*.

What *could* they say, except that he was " Very God and

very man"? that "in him all the fullness of God was pleased to dwell" (Col. 1:19)?

And what, other than this, can *we* say, when through this man we have found unconditional love and the forgiveness of our sin and guilt?

---

## The Nicene Creed

"I believe in one God the Father Almighty, Maker of heaven and earth, and of all things visible and invisible;

"And in one Lord Jesus Christ, the only-begotten Son of God, begotten of His Father before all worlds; God of God; Light of Light; Very God of Very God; Begotten, not made; Being of one substance with the Father, by whom all things were made; Who for us men, and for our salvation, came down from heaven; And was incarnate by the Holy Ghost of the Virgin Mary, and was made man; And was crucified also for us under Pontius Pilate. He suffered and was buried; And the third day He rose again according to the Scriptures; And ascended into heaven; And sitteth on the right hand of the Father. And He shall come again with glory to judge both the quick and the dead; Whose kingdom shall have no end.

"And I believe in the Holy Ghost; The Lord and Giver of Life; Who proceedeth from the Father and the Son; Who with the Father and the Son together is worshiped and glorified; Who spake by the prophets. And I believe one Holy Catholic and Apostolic Church. I acknowledge one Baptism for the remission of sins. And I look for the Resurrection of the dead; and the Life of the world to come. Amen."

## THE GOSPEL OF GOD

Has it ever seemed odd to you that Christianity concerns itself so much with storytelling? The Old Testament is packed with dramatic stories, one following upon another. The Gospels are the story of Jesus. The Acts of the Apostles is a collection of stories about the infant Christian church. When the early apostles set out to carry the Christian faith to the world, they did so by telling a story. Even Jesus himself told stories, illustrating the truth that he brought with one vivid and varied story after another.

This is not accidental. It even can be said that there is something inevitable about it. "Story" is a shortened form of "history." We have seen that the peculiar thing about Christianity is that it roots faith in history. Its unique center is in *what God has done,* in the history that is "his story."

This is not true of other religions. They center in a book, in a system of ideas, in an ethical or moral code, or in mystical or "spiritual" experience. Christianity has its book and knows that it is essential. It puts a high premium upon "beliefs" and "thought." It is supremely concerned with moral purpose and ethical living. And it prizes personal experience of God. But none of these is the center. The center is *God's action in history,* in the life, death, and resurrection of Jesus Christ.

This is why Christianity is a storytelling, or history-telling faith. The " truth " with which it is concerned is truth that cannot be captured in theorems and theories. It is throbbing, living truth, flesh-and-blood truth, for men of flesh and blood. It is truth that emerges as the living God confronts living men where they live.

## Jesus as Teacher

This should be remembered whenever we read the teaching of Jesus. We have repeatedly referred to, and quoted, his " teachings "; but the question of his role as a teacher has been left aside until now. This was done deliberately, because we unavoidably misunderstand the sense in which he was and is our " Teacher " unless we are conscious of *what he did* (the cross) and *who he was* (the incarnation).

It was because there was only a fragmentary consciousness of who he was and of the purpose of his mission that his words were so little understood during his life. As late as the second century the antagonist Celsus was still taunting the Christian church with the fact that even his own disciples had not understood his teachings. This is openly confessed in the Gospels. Again and again his closest followers were confused and perplexed by what he said. At one point he turned to his disciples and asked sadly, " Are you also still without understanding? " (Matt. 15:16).

This was because Jesus was not a " teacher " in the ordinary sense of this word. He did not come primarily to educate or enlighten us, but to redeem and reconcile us to God. Likewise, what we commonly call his " teachings " are not teachings in the ordinary sense. They are inseparably intertwined with what he did and with who he was, and this makes them uniquely different from all other teachings. It is important that we recognize the sense in which they are different.

Ordinary teachings can be separated from their teacher. And their truth or falsity in no way depends upon who does the teaching.

For example, it is obvious that the Pythagorean theorem would be just as true if it had been discovered by Plato rather than by Pythagoras. And it is true for us completely apart from the question of who taught it to us. We would not have found it to be *more* true if we had been taught by Pythagoras himself; and it is not *less* true because we learned it from our tenth-grade schoolteacher.

This is precisely what we cannot say, and must not assume, about the teaching of Jesus. The key that unlocks the door to an understanding of his words is the recognition that they find their truth, and *must* find their truth, in the One who spoke them. This is another way of saying that whereas ordinary teachings are " abstract," his are not. Other teachings may be " abstracted," or " taken away," from their original teacher, and they remain just as true and valuable. If *his* teachings are " abstracted," they either lose their meaning entirely, or they suggest a meaning that is completely different from the one that he intended.

The cruciality of this insight is pointedly illustrated by a recurring refrain in the Gospels. Jesus said: " If any man would come after me, let him deny himself and take up his cross and follow me. For whoever would save his life will lose it, and whoever loses his life for my sake will find it." (Matt. 16:24-25.)

Can this " teaching " be rightly understood apart from the " Teacher " who taught it?

It *can* be understood. It often *is* interpreted without reference to its source. But we should notice that when this is done something very different is said. The words take on a negative hue, and they glorify self-abasement. They lead directly to the idea that self-denial has some special value and virtue in itself. This unavoidably creates the illusion that by some negative pattern of life, by *not* doing certain things, we can fulfill the will of God and " find ourselves."

This is a quite logical interpretation of Jesus' words. It is also a false interpretation. It overlooks the key to his teaching, the fact that his words draw their meaning directly from him. In this " saying " he is not asking us to " deny ourselves." He is asking us to deny ourselves and *follow him* — and this is something quite different. Nor does he say, as is so often said, " Whoever loses his life will find it." What he says is, " Whoever loses his life *for my sake* will find it " — and this is something quite different too.

These words, as do all the words of Jesus, point to *what he did* and *who he was*. They draw their meaning directly from *what has happened* with his appearance on the human scene. Hence we must recognize, and remember, that his teachings are not a collection of " wise sayings " or " timeless truths " — sayings or truths that would be true even if they had been spoken by someone else, and are true without reference to the time and place that they were spoken. On the contrary, here the " teaching " and the " Teacher " are absolutely inseparable. And the " teaching " can be understood only in the light of the cross and the incarnation of the " Teacher."

## The Reign of God

It is because the teaching of Jesus is of this nature that it commonly is called *gospel,* or " the gospel." The Greek word means " glad tidings," or what we today call " good news." The earliest account of his life tells us that he " came into Galilee, preaching the gospel of God " (Mark 1:14). To " preach " is

to " announce," or to " proclaim," something that has happened.

This is the intent of the teaching of Jesus, to announce " the
gospel of God." His basic concern was to bring men into a new
relationship to God, not to teach them new ways of thinking
about God. Thus his message was " news," and not a sym-
posium of new ideas about God. He *announced* the " good
news " that God was acting to redeem and reconcile the world
to himself.

This difference between the purpose and content of his
teaching, and what we ordinarily expect of teachings, might
be compared to the difference between a " spot announcement "
on television and a weekly commentary on the news. A spot
announcement comes at a moment of crisis or emergency. It is
an interruption of the regular routine of telecasting to announce something that has happened. Even the announcement that there is to be an announcement creates in us a
mood of urgency and expectancy.

The weekly commentary on the news is quite different. It
is a more relaxed and leisurely discussion of current issues.
There ordinarily is no mood of excitement and crisis surrounding it. Its quite different purpose is to lead us through a re-
flective examination of our ideas and opinions and possibly
to new conclusions.

This suggests the way in which we must approach and receive the message or teaching of Jesus. It is an " announcement." It came at a moment of crisis — in " the fullness of
time," or when, after centuries of preparation, the time was
" right " or " ripe " for God to invade history. It tells us what
has happened. And when we realize that it is the announcement that God has acted to change our whole relationship to
him, it creates in us a mood of urgency and expectancy.

What is it that has happened? This is what we have been

discussing throughout. The words that Jesus used to encompass this meaning which we find in his life, death, and ressurrection were, "the kingdom of God is at hand."

This phrase "kingdom of God" recurs repeatedly throughout his teaching. It has broad and subtle implications, but its most simple and basic meaning is lucid. The Aramaic language which Jesus spoke (like the Hebrew of his fathers and his Bible) was a dynamic language, one in which words in their simplest meanings generally indicate something active — or something happening — rather than something static. This is true of the word for "kingdom." At its root it means "reign" or "rule." The "kingdom of God" is the *reign* of God, as the Sovereign of the world and of human history.

What Jesus was proclaiming, then, was that with his appearance in history the reign of God was "at hand." He was announcing that a world that was in anarchy and rebellion, and enslaved to "principalities and powers," would now be set free to live under, and to serve, its rightful Sovereign.

If this *is* the "good news" of Christ, then why is it that two thousand years later we still are so obviously in need of this redemption? If he came to announce that God has reconciled the world to himself, why is the world not reconciled to him?

The answer is (and we shall need to think the answer through) : the world *is* reconciled, even though it *is not*.

Each of these two themes is present throughout the teaching of Jesus, as each is echoed in the whole of the New Testament. The reign of God "*has* come"; but we must look in hope to the day when it "*will* come." The Kingdom of God is here; but we still must pray, "Thy kingdom come." We *are* forgiven, although we live every hour in desperate need of God's forgiveness. We *are* redeemed, even though we remain sinners in dire need of Christ's redemption.

It is necessary that we see how each of these is true. It is only as we see the truth of each, and can put them together, that we understand the situation into which we are thrust by our faith in Christ.

If we parallel our situation in life and history to the situation at the close of a war, it helps us to see how each side can be — and is — true. The Phillips' version paraphrases some words of Paul, in which he describes the " good news " which Jesus brought, thus: " He came and told both you who were far from God and we who were near that the war was over." (Eph. 2:17.)

We all have read of men being killed in a war when the war actually was over. Before the days of modern communications, it was not unusual for a war to continue after it had ended. The enemy would be defeated and would concede defeat. A treaty of peace would be drafted and signed, in the palace of the king, bringing the war to an end. It then would be weeks, or even months, before the couriers would arrive at the outermost frontiers of the fighting with the news (the *good* news!) that the war was over.

In the meantime the battle continued on its bloody way. Every hour was just as crisis-laden as if the war had not been won. Peace was established, but the fighting could not cease. And for every man involved each day of fighting was in the most literal sense a matter of life and death.

This suggests the way in which we must understand the announcement of Jesus that the reign of God has come. And it indicates the kind of situation in which we live, if we live as Christians. We live " between the times." The war is over; but it continues, and we must continue fighting.

This means, on the one hand, that the reign of God *has* come. " The kingdom of God has come upon you," Jesus said. (Luke 11:20.) Peace *has* been established. God *has* reconciled us to himself through the life and death of Christ. We saw in Chapter 3 that this is a "finished work," and that the fact that it *is* a finished work is the fundamental fact of our faith. This is why Paul can say with profoundest joy, and without qualification, "There is therefore now no condemnation for those who are in Christ Jesus" (Rom. 8:1). We *are* forgiven; our guilt *is* overcome; our slavery to sin *is* broken; God *has* reconciled us to himself, and given us a "peace . . . which passes all understanding."

On the other hand, we live on the "front lines" of human existence. The world has not heard the "good news," and we have believed it only intermittently and in part. Thus the war continues and must continue. We must contend with the tyranny of our sin every day, in just as serious and real a way as though that tyranny had not been broken. Our guilt threatens daily to conquer and destroy our freedom just as though it had not been overcome. In every way the war continues, and we must fight with life-and-death seriousness.

## The Movement of Repentance

If this *is* the two-sided truth about our situation, and if each side must be taken with equal seriousness, what does the victory of Christ, his life, death, and resurrection, mean to our lives here and now? A full reply to this question would have to be as broad and deep as Christian experience; but the heart of the answer is easily identified in the New Testament. The words that Jesus used to indicate it are "repentance" and "faith."

The movement of repentance profoundly alters our situation in human life by permitting us to be ourselves. It cancels out the nerve-wracking necessity to play little games of pretense, with ourselves, with others, or with God.

Franz Kafka, a perplexing twentieth-century Czechoslo-
vakian novelist, wrote a queer little story that he called *Meta-
morphosis*. It is the tale of a man who awoke one morning
to discover that during the night he had turned into a huge
cockroach. Kafka gives us a detailed chronicle of the man's
trials and tribulations as he lives his brief span as a cockroach,
and then of his pathetic and tragic end.

The most striking overtone of this peculiar story is that
although all of this man's frantic efforts to turn himself back
into an acceptable human being are completely futile, he cannot accept this fact. He knows what he should be, and he
knows that he is not what he should be. There is nothing that
he can do about it, but he keeps assuring himself that there is.
He repeatedly fails, and writhes in anxiety and frustration as
he fails. But then he immediately tries again — to fail again.

The end of the story finds him exactly where he was at the
beginning, still a cockroach — except that on the final page
he is a dead cockroach.

This is the vicious circle of our lives. We resolve that we
will change; and we fail in our attempt to do so. We make a
new vow to change, and this is followed by a new failure.
Each new failure adds new guilt for having failed, and our
new failures with their new guilt are the only *really* new
thing in our lives. This circle of resolve and failure is broken
only by death — except as it is broken by the movement of
repentance.

Luther once received a letter from Staupitz, his close friend
and counselor, that said: "I have promised God a thousand
times that I would become a better man, but I never kept my
promise. I am not going to make any more vows. Experience
has taught me that I cannot keep them. Unless God is merciful to me for Christ's sake, and grants me a new departure,
I shall not be able to stand before him."

Luther's comment was that this is " God-pleasing despair."
It also is the door to the " new life " that Christ promises. In
one sense all that Christ asks of us is simply that we *be ourselves* before God. Of course, this *is* an experience of despair,
because when we are honest about ourselves before the holy
God we immediately must acknowledge that we have nothing
to offer him but our sin and our failures.

But this is precisely what Christ asks us to offer God, in
honest confession. (Reread the story at the conclusion of Chapter 2.) It is only by being ourselves, or by making this movement of " God-fearing despair " and honest confession, that
we open ourselves to the redemptive power of the cross and
the " new life " that it offers us.

This is what Christ meant by repentance. After he had
announced that " the kingdom of God is at hand," his first
word was " repent." (Mark 1:15.) To repent is to cease " play
acting " and throw ourselves on the mercy of God. It is a
movement in which we turn our backs on our way of rebellion,
relying wholly upon his forgiveness and love. In this movement the vicious circle of resolve and failure is broken, to be
replaced by the circle of repentance and faith and the new life
that this brings.

We should notice that this movement of repentance is
made possible by the cross. Apart from a sense of what Christ
did in giving his life for us, we cannot repent. Where we can
see no way out, we will not accept the fact that we are what
we are. Nor can we confess the truth about ourselves to God.
Rather, we pull our cloak of hypocrisy and pretense closer
about us and " play-act " — in the futile, frustrating attempt
to convince ourselves, others, and God that we really are not
what we are (or, at least, will not be for long).

It is the " good news " that God has given us through the
cross that permits us to be ourselves *before* him, and to pre-

sent our unvarnished selves *to* him. When we see that Christ
has "taken our place," and that through Christ's sacrifice of
his life God is holding out to us unconditional forgiveness and
love, we can turn and accept this forgiveness and love *in spite
of* our complete unworthiness of it. To do so is to repent.

It is crucial to recognize that this repentance which Christ
asks of us is not something that we should, or must, do once.
It cannot even be said that it is something that we must do
frequently. This is the rhythm of the Christian life. The
movement of repentance and faith — replacing the movement
of resolve and failure — is the continuous movement of Christian living.

### The Gift of Faith

This is why "faith" is for Protestants the central word in
the Christian vocabulary. It also is why it is so tragic that this
is perhaps the most frequently misunderstood of the essential
Christian words. It is misinterpreted in several ways, but each
can be traced to a single error: a failure to recognize that a
Christian can speak the word "faith" correctly only if, as he
speaks, he is pointing to the Christ of the cross.

There are three ingredients in Christian faith, each necessary to the others.

1. The first is *belief*. When Jesus had proclaimed that the
reign of God is "at hand," he said, "Repent, and *believe* in
the gospel" (Mark 1:15). This is a necessary element of Christian faith: believing, or hearing and accepting the "good
news" that God has acted decisively in the life, death, and
resurrection of Jesus Christ to redeem us and reconcile us to
himself and to one another.

2. A second ingredient is *trust*. Belief is a crucial and necessary element of Christian faith. But it can have little signifi-

cant effect in our lives unless we are prepared, *as* we believe, to trust ourselves to God. We can believe one way and live another (as people who read books like this frequently do). We can even accept the entire gamut of Christian doctrine and remain essentially unchanged (as people who write books like this frequently do). This obviously is not what Christ meant by faith. As the little letter of James pointedly remarks, " even the demons believe " (ch. 2:19).

Christian faith requires reliance, or confidence, to be Christian faith. If we are to respond to Christ's call, we must trust our lives to God through him. With each movement of faith we must forsake our campaign to override God's will and remake ourselves in our own image. Paul called this turning-in-trust, the movement of repentance and faith, " the confidence that we have through Christ toward God." It is to know and to acknowledge, in act as well as in word, that we are in no way " sufficient of ourselves to claim anything as coming from us," and that in the most literal sense " our sufficiency is from God " (II Cor. 3:5).

3. Even full belief and total trust are not necessarily Christian faith, however. It is only as *Christ* is the content of our faith, or only when we believe his " good news," and trust what he has done and will do for us, that we move into Christian faith.

This is why we must always remember that Christian faith is a gift and in no sense an achievement or an accomplishment. We can, by an act of the will, believe many things *about* Christ, but this is not faith *in* Christ. We can trust by a resolve to trust; but if it is not trust in what Christ did and does for us, this is not Christian faith. It is only as God gives himself to us in Christ, and Christ becomes the object of our belief and the ground of our trust, that we have Christian faith.

Once more, we must say this because it is the cross that makes faith in God through Christ possible. It is an axiom of all pagan religion (ancient *and* modern) that "God has dealings only with the pure." This is a conviction that is in-grained within us, what we *must* assume apart from the cross. We cannot believe that the holy God will have "dealings" with us except as we manage to create in some fashion the illusion that we are, or will be, "pure."

Thus it is as we look to the cross that Christian faith be-comes possible. We discover in the cross that God's forgiveness and love are unconditional . . . that he has entered into the very fabric of our lives to reconcile us to himself . . . and that what he requires of us, in order that we may be reconciled to him, is only that we accept the gift of redemption which he offers us through Christ. It is then that we realize, as Kierke-gaard has expressed it, that "the opposite of sin is not virtue, but faith." And we find that we *can* believe and trust, for in giving us Christ God gives us both the ground of our trust and the will to believe in him.

This leads to an amazing discovery. We find that "faith" actually is the most *practical* word in the Christian vocabulary.

Jesus once said, "With God all things are possible" (Matt. 19:26). It is faith that makes "all things" possible, all of the things that are impossible when we are vibrating between our resolutions and our failures, chained to our sin and guilt. In the movement of faith we suddenly understand the famous prayer of Augustine: "O God, give what thou demandest, and demand what thou wilt." We discover that as God gives us Christ he gives a redemptive power that makes possible a "new life," a life of obedience to him and of forgiving love with one another.

It is important that we recognize that this redemptive power which makes our new life possible is not, and can never be regarded as, a possession. Any claim, explicit or implicit, that we " have " what God wishes us to have, or " are " what God demands that we be, is the rebirth of our old self, not a reflection of the new. In the area of self-estimate and self-judgment Karl Barth has said what must be said: " Rightly understood, there are no Christians; there is only the eternal opportunity of becoming Christian." We can claim nothing — except what Christ has done for us. And we should remember that Jesus did *not* say, " All things are possible." What he said is, " *With God* all things are possible."

But he *did* say, " With God *all things are possible.*" Pessimism before the question of the possibility of obedience to God, and of genuine good in human life and history, has no place in Christian thinking. This is true, however, neither because of a naïve underestimate of the power and persistence of sin and evil, nor because of a dreamy overestimate of human potentiality. It is true for one reason, and one reason only: because God has come, and comes, to us in Christ.

Emil Brunner has remarked that " the state of the Christian is one of ' confident despair.' But this despair is *confident.*" We must accord each side its proper and equal weight. In the presence of Christ and his " great accusation," we cannot forget that " all have sinned and fall short of the glory of God " (Rom. 3:23). Neither can we forget that his message is " *good news,*" that he died to set us free, and that the redemptive power of his presence in our lives is both our possibility and God's will for us.

### REFERENCES

In this volume quotations from the following publications, listed in the order of their appearance, are used by permission:

Aldous Huxley, *Those Barren Leaves*. Harper & Brothers. Copyright, 1925, by Aldous Huxley. Used by permission of Harper Brothers. (Pages 361–362 in Avon Publications edition.)

Stefan George, quoted in *Nietzsche: Philosopher, Psychologist, Antichrist,* by Walter A. Kaufmann. Princeton University Press, 1950. Page 11. Used by permission of the publisher.

Norman Mailer, *The Deer Park*. G. P. Putnam's Sons. Copyright, 1955, by Norman Mailer. Used by permission of G. P. Putnam's Sons. (Page 12 in Signet Books edition.)

Herbert H. Farmer, *God and Men*. James Nisbet & Co., Ltd., London. Pages 190–191. Used by permission.

W. H. Auden, "For the Time Being, A Christmas Oratorio," Random House, Inc. Copyright, 1944, by W. H. Auden. Used by permission of Random House, Inc. (Page 60 in *Religious Drama/1*, Meridian Books edition.)

Gabriel Marcel, " A Man of God " in *A Man of God, Ariadne, The Funeral Pyre*. Secker and Warburg, Ltd., 1952. Pages 47, 53, 59. Used by permission of Secker and Warburg, Ltd.

# THE MEANING OF CHRIST

The English philosopher C. E. M. Joad once exclaimed: "Thank God for e Church of England. It's the only thing that saves us—from Christianity." lthough Joad's statement is extreme (he later joined the Church of England), any readers of this book (THE MEANING OF CHRIST) may suspect that other urches have been guilty of saving people from a dynamic encounter with the essage of the New Testament. The author opens his discussion of "the mean-g of Christ" by stressing the fact that words in themselves are meaningless, cept as they are associated in our minds with some thing or some one. The ord "God" for the church has always drawn its content by association with e carpenter from Nazareth, Jesus. When we give our undivided attention to hat he has to say to us, it becomes apparent that to talk as he did about human ture is not the best way "to win friends and influence people." Indeed, he oves to be the great Accuser of mankind! Yet this is only a half-truth, for r author goes on to point out that Jesus not only unmasks the hypocrisy of man beings, but also reveals that the love of God is in no way withdrawn om mankind in spite of its unlovableness.

The mystery of Jesus consists in this twofold revelation that he brings—the velation of man's unworthiness and of God's love for man in spite of this worthiness. The creeds of the early church, which are the common possession Roman, Reformed, and Orthodox Christianity, were hammered out not to plain but to maintain the mystery of this twofold revelation which comes to us Jesus Christ.

The concluding chapter on "The Gospel of God" brings into focus what this eaning of Christ involves for Christian men and women as they live out their ves from day to day in the twentieth century.

## DISCUSSION STARTERS

scussion I. Chapter 1. The Christian church insists that the word "God" can rightly understood only as we focus our attention on the first-century car-nter, Jesus of Nazareth.

1. Words, when you think about it, *are* mysterious. How do the sounds we ll words convey meaning from one person to another?

2. A very basic Biblical idea is "monotheism." It is possible that focusing on sus may be a threat to monotheism. How?

3. What does the word "understand" mean? Does it mean the same thing in ience as in religion? What is the "optical problem" that we face as Christians?

scussion II. Chapter 2. Jesus throws a searchlight on human nature so pene-ating that it reveals to mankind the most depressing news ever heard by man ears.

1. In view of what is said in this chapter, the word "good" receives a new eaning from Jesus. Contrast Jesus' definition of this word with its popular usage.

2. Was Jesus crucified because the people of the first century were particularly uel or were the emotions of hostility that he aroused in his contemporaries rt and parcel of the equipment of human nature in every generation? How uld you explain this to a humanist?

3. What, according to Jesus, is the worst form that man's rebellion against od takes?

***Discussion III. Chapter 3.*** Jesus throws a searchlight on God's nature so pene-trating that it reveals to mankind the most joyful news ever to penetrat human ears.

1. People are often guilty without "feeling" guilty; they often "feel" guilt when they are not guilty. How is this possible?

2. What is the parable of the prodigal God? How is God's extravaganc revealed in the cross?

3. Why is it more difficult to accept forgiveness than to give it?

***Discussion IV. Chapter 4.*** The claim that Jesus is both fully human and full divine is a *mystery* defended by the church from very early in its history. Th creeds of the church were not drawn up to *explain* this mystery, but only maintain it.

1. What did John Calvin mean when he said that creeds should be sung an not said?

2. List some examples of statements about Jesus that show that his humanit is denied—and some that indicate that his deity is denied.

***Discussion V. Chapter 5.*** The knowledge of God that Jesus Christ has reveale to us makes it possible for us to be ourselves before God; the knowledge ourselves that Jesus Christ has shown us makes it necessary for us to ask Go to change the selves we now see ourselves to be.

1. Can we understand what Jesus said without taking into consideration wh he was?

2. Using the author's analogy of the end of a war, how is it possible to spea of God's victory already being won, and at the same time "yet to come"?

3. What is the difference between a life motivated by "resolve and failur and one propelled by "repentance and faith"?

4. What are the three ingredients in Christian faith?

## Study Suggestions

This book may be covered in five periods, one for each chapter. If mo sessions can be scheduled, two periods could be devoted to Chs. 2; 3; 4; or

*This Study Guide was prepared by Robert P. Montgomery, university paste Princeton University, Princeton, N. J.*